MW01088591

Peace in the Meadow

and other encounters with *life*

by Ilene Smith

Forward Movement Publications, Cincinnati

© 1988. Forward Movement Publications, 412 Sycamore Street, Cincinnati, Ohio 45202-4195. Printed in U.S.A.

Introduction

My own little piece of ground in the north country is called the Bittersweet Garden. It is quite an ordinary place, at least until you see the gold and scarlet of bittersweet burning against October's brilliant blue sky. Or the soft pink of an old-fashioned moss rose gently dropping its petals to the ground, or lilac flowers drooping heavily on their stems.

For many years I lived in a sturdy old farmhouse surrounded by 132 acres of beautiful rural countryside. Since last fall I have lived in a small cabin on an acre of land taken from the southwest corner of the farm. It was built a few years ago, and here I have planted my bittersweet and some of my gardens, especially the strawberry beds. Now I have moved to the cabin and the rest of the farm has been sold. Some of the meditations were written at the farmhouse which will always have a special place in my heart, but my cabin is a beloved home to me now. Truly, in our father's house there are many mansions—and fields, and streams, woods and *meadows.*

Ilene Smith
Autumn 1988

Peace in the Meadow

When the wild strawberry moon was waxing full in June, I repaired to a meadow where I have found large, sweet berries for several years. It is a good meadow but the hay crop is poor now—plowing and reseeding is needed. Meanwhile, the wild strawberries do best in just such a field where the hay is thin, and there are wildflowers—daisies, hawkweed, yarrow, and heal-all to keep them company. Lira, my dog, Jasper and Altoona, my cats, all go along to keep me company and to have a little excitement, chasing butterflies and all sorts of imaginary meadow mice and birds. A small spring-fed stream is beginning its long journey to the Atlantic Ocean nearby and is handy in case anyone becomes thirsty. I become so engrossed in finding the gleaming red berries down in the meadow grass that I forget almost everything else. I feel the warm, gentle, lonesome wind that plays over the meadow. I hear the hum of bees and I smell the fragrant berries, but mostly I am lost in a summer's reverie.

But then I straighten up for a minute to admire the snowy white clouds floating around up in the sky and come face to face with a coyote who is just topping the rise where I have been picking. This is the New England coyote who picked up some wolf genes in Canada while moving into the northeast. He is larger than the grayish western coyote. His coat is a beautiful blend of tawny golden brown and black and rust colors. He is so beautiful, so free, so wild. I wonder if he and Lira will get into a fight or if he will chase the cats. But Lira wags her tail, the cats are gamboling around as usual on these excursions, and the coyote looks at us for a moment with his grave, watchful, light yellow eyes and turning, trots off in another direction. I hope he, too, finds heavy clusters of the bright red, yellow-flecked berries and has a safe and good summer. The meadow is big enough for us all and I am glad to have been companioned even for a moment by such an interesting animal.

1

I know that almost anyone would ask me if I hadn't been "afraid." But I don't think any of us, including the coyote was afraid. It was just good to be out in a lovely sunlit meadow, finding healthy wild food, hearing the soft whistling wail of an upland plover, and bubbling song of a bob-o-link.

> Wolves and sheep will live
> together in peace,
> and leopards will lie down
> with young goats.
> Calves and lion cubs will feed
> together,
> and little children will take
> care of them.

Isaiah 11:6

Empty Nest

In the dimness under the pines I came across the empty nest of a ruffled grouse, commonly called partridge by country people. I can not help admiring the lovely accomodations this little forest bird had for her burgeoning family. Overhead the pine needles, hot in the sunshine, fill the air with a resinous fragrance. On the forest floor it is cool and there are fresh green ferns, and mossy logs adorned with pixies cup lichens and soft green mosses. The nest itself is simply a partridge-sized hollow tight up against a pine tree in a deep layer of dry pine needles on the southwestern side. It is full of empty egg shells now, a pale glossy beige in color, most of the halves neatly tucked into each other by the mother bird, the same as I usually do with my breakfast egg shells. Some pieces lie around outside the nest which is not far from a woods road.

What a lovely place for the little bird to brood and hatch out her babies, the father partridge keeping watch not too far off, ready to distract any intruders who might appear.

2

Partridge babies are downy feathered, steady on their toes and bright-eyed as soon as they are hatched and dried off in the summer breezes. So, immediately after hatching the mother bird leads her little flock away from the nest. I know that even now they are out there somewhere on the forest floor or in the wild apple thickets and she is teaching them the proper partridge lifestyle. They will learn about taking dust baths in little finely sifted dirt wallows along the old road, about the delicious flavor of ants and other bugs, how to properly savor the taste of fresh strawberries and all of the other foods available everywhere for the partridge family. And eventually how to make that heart-stopping bang when they fly away from trespassers in their domain, such as hikers and hunters.

How thoughtfully placed the nest was. There just happened to be some pine branches on the woods floor surrounding it, dropped there by the tree farmer while doing some trimming work. These would keep off any casual predator that might wander too close. Secure on her nest, the mother bird brooded her eggs, serene and peaceful as the woods itself.

Now the nest is empty and deserted but, charming as it is, I know that the wise little mother bird would not want to reverse time, corral the baby birds and crowd them back into the nest. They were meant to grow and learn and become part of the woods that they love; that is their inheritance. It is the same with us. Sometimes we wish we could go backward in time, and wipe out all the bad choices, unwise decisions, unkind words and deeds that we have been responsible for, and start all over again.

But probably it is just as well that we are unable to do this. We learn through difficulty, adversity and failure as much as we learn through success and happiness. If we can get away from our preoccupation with sitting among the bean husks in a far country and return like the Prodigal Son to our Father we can have a fresh start in life with Him. He sees us when we are still a long way from home, surrounds us with his loving care and helps us to live a new life—more faithful, more loving, more worthwhile than the old.

For this son of mine was dead, but now he is alive, he was lost, but now he has been found.

Luke 15:24

Moth Mullein

I was walking in the meadow near my cabin in the early evening when I saw several plants of moth mullein—*beautiful* moth mullein, as I always think of it. And *mysterious* moth mullein, for the plants had endured being cut with the meadow grasses for hay, but here it was grown up again, its lovely blossoms a soft moth-like white with a pinkish tinge, especially in the very heart where it shades into a deep rose color; and bright orange anthers shine like stars in the mysterious little flowers.

I first saw this plant growing rather sparsely (I have never found very many of these flowers in one place and those only rarely) in a lovely, small meadow fenced by stone walls in an area some distance from here where my sister and I were taking a walk on a tree-shaded, beckoning old road, and turned into the meadow just a bit through a barway we noticed. At the time, I thought my sister would be with me forever to share my life and the outdoors we both loved. There was heartache and sadness instead, and she died a few years ago. But when I see lovely moth mullein standing so quietly, so silently, its petals full of an infinitely gentle luminescent quality—there is a fleeting thought of the years that might have been, lost years, perhaps, to me, but not to the searching, loving heart of God to whom I long ago entrusted her.

What we see now is like a dim image in a mirror; then we shall see face-to-face.

1 Corinthians 13:12

4

Good Weather

Today the heat was intense, but it is time for the wild red raspberries to be ripening in my own little secret raspberry patch down the old road. So I put Lira in the car and we drive down the road as far as the tree farm where I park the car and then we walk on, to a lovely, shaded, mysterious glen. Alongside the glen is my berry patch and I pick several pints of the fragrant, juicy, red berries that are hanging heavily on the bushes now. They are dead ripe and fall off at only a touch down into the leaves and debris on the ground, so I have to pick carefully.

I find that my berry patch isn't so "secret" after all. There are trampled paths through it and a clump of black hair caught on some brambles hints that Black Bear loves this patch, too. And now I know that those dug-up jack-in-the-pulpit plants which I found in the woods the other day were also indicators of Black Bear's presence. For he is the only animal I know of who has a fond gastronomic regard for the wrinkled flat bulbs of this interesting wild flower. The bulbs contain crystals of calcium oxalate that affect a human tongue something like a mixture of sulfuric acid and powdered glass. But Black Bear thinks they are just fine. After filling the berry containers, Lira and I go down into the glen and rest awhile.

The glen has a coolness, almost bordering on coldness, no matter how hot the day, and it is a great relief from the sultry heat of the raspberry clearing. A stream can be found in the upper reaches of the glen, but in some unfathomable way which as yet I have been unable to discover, it disappears underground and there is a dry stream bed in its lower reaches. The dry stream bed goes under the old road and then there is a precipitous rocky gorge. If you look down, or laboriously climb down, you will find the water, back in sight, again forming a quiet, deep woodland pool and soon after joining the main creek. Resting in the coolness of the gorge, I become aware that a nest of flicker infants has just outgrown their quarters and made their entrance into a bigger world. There

5

are a good many anxious "wick-a-wick-a-wicks" as the parents feed their scattered fledglings and try without much success to keep things as orderly as they were when the babes fit in the nest. It's an exciting afternoon for the flickers, and if I had not been abroad in the heat of the day I would not have been able to watch them quietly or see the mother flicker tuck a bright red Juneberry into the mouth of one of her offspring. Then I climb down to the pool at the base of the gorge and find a lovely old bottle dating, I would guess, from the very earliest days of marketing Coca-Cola. It is a very pale, delicate sea green, unmarred in any way. I admire the artistic Coca-Cola lettering, the legend "Watertown, N.Y." on the bottom, the heaviness of the bottle. I will take it home and set it on the pine shelf near my writing table. It is not uncommon to find some lovely old relic here, for passersby on the now unused road above apparently often halted their buggies or, perhaps later, cars and tossed odds and ends down to the foot of the gorge.

Then Lira and I return home after a pleasant, rewarding trip, even though the heat is stifling.

It makes me think of other times when I have been abroad in inclement weather and been rewarded beyond measure. There was the fierce March blizzard when out of the storm a beautiful Lark Bunting started up from the meadow edge flying off into the stinging snowflakes singing loudly its sweet trilling spring song. This is a Great Plains bird, with only seven or eight very rare sightings in this state, and I had never seen one before. Another bitter cold early winter's morning, about 20 degrees below or so, when I took Lira out for her walk before day had quite dawned, I heard a nestling sound and a horned lark that had been sleeping for the night, resting on a frayed tattered bit of cornstalk in the cornfield, flew off over the meadows. I learned a bit more about the birds and how they manage when the weather is very severe.

One springtime when the creek was in a turbulent, wild flood I happened to walk by and noticed a pair of mergansers in these tumultuous waters. I had never seen them before,

6

but there they were, diving through the waves, mounting on their wings for short low flights in the flying spray, having a really marvelous time, although it seemed to me that they should be more cautious of the fierce current.

And then there was the little sparrow-hawk the other day. The wind was at gale force; indeed it brought down many trees all over the area. But the little hawk would fly a bit and then hover in one spot even though the wind was beating against him so fiercely. This was his moment of glory. You could see that it was great for him, his chance to test his powers of flight against the strongest of gales.

It all makes me wonder if we humans are really intended for a life of continual calmness and security. We do not really know. Perhaps God made us, too, to be part of wild, stormy days and poor weather as well as peaceful days of safe harborage. At least I know I have seen some beautiful exultant things while out in some very inclement weather that I would never have known about if I had always kept close to my hearth and only went abroad on "good days."

Of course I admit one can overdo this. Some years ago when I had a faithful beloved dog named Fido, I took him on a hike up into the nearby hills. A terrible lightning and thunder storm came up unexpectedly and the only shelter available was one corner of a mostly fallen-down sugar shanty. It was snug and dry there, but Fido, who did not fancy electrical storms, cast many a reproachful glance my way. Finally the electrical aspect of the storm abated and we made our way home in one of the most drenching downpours I have ever seen. It took quite a while for Fido to regain his confidence in me as a walking companion.

> *Be merciful to me, O God, be merciful*
> *because I come to you for safety.*
> *In the shadow of your wings I*
> *find protection*
> *until the raging storms are over.*

Psalm 57:1

Keeping Busy

Several miles upstream from my cabin there is a place where one of the branches of the creek finds its way through a culvert beneath a little rough dirt road. This is hilly wild country and some beaver came along, found it well suited to their needs, and settled there. Noticing that the roadway was higher than the stream that went through the culvert beneath it, they took a shortcut in their usual dam-building procedures and used the road as their dam. Then all they had to do was to plug the culvert (the leak in the dam, as the beaver saw it) with mud, sticks, stones and other debris. This caused a predictable backup of water, making a fine pond for the beaver lodge, and also flooding the dirt road.

For a while, road workers cleared out the culvert every day and then every night the beaver faithfully plugged up the culvert again. This isolated quiet spot became a really busy place with modifications to the terrain taking place both day and night. Eventually, however, the town road workers devised a solution that made everyone happy. They brought in a truckload or two of flattish stones, and with a grade-all, they placed the stones in a neat row across the brook a few yards back from the disputed culvert and roadway.

The beaver obligingly saw the possibilities in this structural work, and plugged all of the openings between the stones. The result was a fine new dam which kept their pond at a convenient level and the overflow went back into the stream and through the culvert with no more road flooding. This seemed to me to be the generous, loving type of thinking that would appeal to St. Francis. In most such beaver flooding situations in this state or elsewhere all sorts of threats and complaints are made against the beaver. Trapping seasons and limits are often extended and sometimes there is live trapping and removal of the beaver to some distant area.

The little water animals instinctively know that one of the reasons God placed them on earth is to do the hydraulic work necessary to slow down turbulent streams, making nice ponds brimming full of water for the local wildlife. Eventually, by way of natural succession, the beaver flows (ponds) will become fertile beaver meadows, much prized by the people who till the earth. Dams, ponds, lodges and diversion ditches are all just part of a good night's work for the beaver.

Then God commanded, let the water be filled with many kinds of living beings, and let the air be filled with birds. So God created the great sea monsters, all kinds of creatures that live in the water, and all kinds of birds. And God was pleased with what he saw.

Genesis 1:20-21

In the Shadows

Along one section of my lovely rippling creek there is a great, very old hemlock tree. The other hemlocks around seem young and untried in comparison. There are limestone ledges at the base of the tree where I love to sit, leaning against this mighty dispenser of shade, oxygen and fragrant resins. It must be very old to have attained such size and I give thanks that it somehow escaped charcoal burners, potash makers, tannery suppliers and lumberjacks, and is here now where Lira and I can rest in its shadow.

I renew my own strength from my closeness to this lovely tree that has stood steadfast for so many years. Troubles and difficulties seem less vexing here in the filtered dimness beneath the kindly hemlock. There is a hollow in it and signs that is has been often used by raccoon families, and where could they find a more suitable home than deep within the sturdy trunk of this tree? The brook which the babies will learn to follow all of their days mumbles pleasantly past the rock ledges where I sit.

As I lean my face against the deeply ridged bark I suddenly notice that at a height several feet above my head there is a very old barbed wire that almost goes through the very heart of this beautiful old tree. In its youth someone must have carelessly used it in place of a fence post. The tree sealed off with new growth and healing resins the injury that could have been an avenue for serious insect and fungal invasion. Instead of dying it thrived and continued to grow, offering shade, shelter and comfort to those who wander by. And from the tree I learn that we do not need to be destroyed by hurts, troubles, disappointments or poor health. God can heal us and perhaps the scars will help us to find real life—everlasting life.

The people of Israel will have nothing more to do with idols; I will answer their prayers and take care of them. Like an evergreen tree I will shelter them; I am the source of all their blessings.

Hosea 14:8

A Washtub Full of Black-Eyed Susans

Black-Eyed Susans have always been one of my very favorite wildflowers. They originally were a western prairie flower, but are gradually moving eastward. I have only found them in small quantities along the local roadsides, abandoned meadows and other bits of so-called wasteland. Sometimes I would pick just a single flower and carry it home to put in one of my antique cream bottles, on a window sill. There I would admire the sun shining through the deep gold of the petals held together by the lovely warm brown heart of the flower. Other times I just enjoyed them without any picking at all.

So, accustomed to this frugal traffic in Black-Eyed Susans, I was reduced to a state of astonished speechlessness one summer day when a friend drove up and began to unload what seemed like hundreds of Black-Eyed Susan flowers from his pickup. "Do you like Black-Eyed Susans?" he asked rather hesitantly. (Perhaps he was afraid I would not want to bother with them!) "Black-Eyed Susans," I breathed in wonder, gathering as many of them in my arms as possible. "I love them and I've just never had enough to suit me." And I gazed at them in amazement. I could not believe that anyone would trouble themselves to pick all those flowers just for me.

Well, it turned out that they weren't exactly "picked." My friend had been driving to Barnes Corners, a small town on the western edge of the Tug Hill Plateau, when he came up behind a town road workman who was mowing the roadside. A great swath of these lovely flowers was left lying in the warm sunshine behind the machine. He stopped, gathering up as many as he could and brought them to me, for he knew I loved wildflowers.

There was a problem of what to put them in, but finally I remembered the old-fashioned washtub in the woodshed, a rather homely laundry relic from the days when a wash day was really a wash day. Filled with fresh water and Black-Eyed Susans I think it would have taken first in any flower show. My priceless gift—these lovely lonely roadside flowers; if I can just hold this moment! I know there will be times when I will feel lonesome, misused, overlooked, unloved, and miserable things will happen to me. Then if I can only remember the Black-Eyed Susans, bright country flowers grown in a roadside ditch, and the day that it was hard to find anything big enough to hold them all.

Each one of us has received a special gift in proportion to what Christ has given. As the scripture says,
> *When he went up to the very heights,*
> *he took many captives with him;*
> *he gave gifts to mankind.*

Ephesians 4:7

11

Summer Squash

Summer squash is something that grows on one, so to speak. I have never been able to resist planting a few hills of them in the garden. For one thing they are so attractive—the huge golden blossoms and then the pale yellow squash sheltering under the big, thrifty-looking, green leaves in the garden. They are about the only thing that grows for me with no coaxing, no spraying, no special horticultural extravaganzas except a little judicious hoeing and weeding. They impart a productive, business-like atmosphere to my garden, suggesting that here is a gardener who is not just putting in her time. Then, too, the "little people" can have nice afternoon tea parties under the shady leaves. (I found this out from my mother who was very adept at entertaining her children with stories when we complained that we had "nothing to do.")

When young and tender, in the fingerling stage, the skin of the squash can be punctured with a fingernail and they are just right. At first I simply slice them up, boil, drain and add a little butter, pepper and salt. A bit later on I may dip the slices in a mixture of egg and flour and fry them. Prepared in either of these ways, the squash is delightful, but it is a slow way to use up a lot of squash, which is exactly what I have.

I do not have an aggressive enough demeanor to make it possible for me to give away much summer squash. (You would be surprised at the excuses people can think of for refusing to accept them as gifts—"I'm taking the first plane out for Hawaii in the morning!") If I do manage to give a few away I am assailed by dark suspicions that they will eventually be *thrown out.*

So, one July recently, surrounded by baskets, dishpans, kettles and paper sacks overflowing with summer squash, I decided to experiment with developing a really fine casserole dish that would not only use up lots of squash, but encourage one to really "make a meal" of this pleasant vegetable, so summery and light, full of the usual vitamins found in yellow vegetables.

With some pride I record the final results. It is easy to make, very tasty, I think, and does not rely on any hard-to-get ingredients. Also, it goes well with almost anything else that might be on the menu, and is very helpful to the busy gardener who wants to see everything *used.*

Yellow Squash Casserole

5 cups squash that has been boiled 10 minutes and drained
1 cup fine whole wheat cracker crumbs (Crush with a rolling pin)
¼ cup cooked chicken livers, finely cut
¼ cup pieces of cooked bacon, finely cut
¼ cup Velveeta cheese, cut up
1 tablespoon wheat germ
1 teaspoon dill seed
salt and pepper to flavor

Mix these ingredients together and bake about 30 minutes at 350 degrees in a covered dish or until done.

Fields, don't be afraid,
but be joyful and glad
because of all the Lord has
done for you.

Joel 2:21

The Lilies of the Field and L. L. Bean

In early summer there is a lovely, stately flower that blooms in wet meadows and damp swales. It is the Canada lily, whose pale, tawny orange flowers in the shape of little witches' caps hang over the wild swamp grasses. They are often visited by hummingbirds who probably think that someone planted them just for their benefit, and probably they are right. This is a native American lily, so it could not be the variety that Jesus was referring to when he spoke of "the lilies of the field. . . they toil not neither do they spin but Solomon in all his glory was not arrayed like one of these."

That is so true. Even with all of the financial resources of Solomon's court, the natural beauty of God's handiwork could not be duplicated. If it was hopeless for Solomon, it is even more hopeless for me, and I pick up much of my attire from rummage sales.

Sometimes I go merely to buy anything that will fit and is useable, but early this summer I had a definite objective in mind when I attended our church rummage sale. The kindly, sensible lady who heads up these sales asked me if there was anything in particular that I wanted. "Yes, there is," I replied. "I need to paint one side of my house this summer and I'd like an old ragged shirt that I could wear without worrying about dripping paint on it. Afterwards, I could just throw it away." "Here's just the thing," she responded, reaching into a pile of clothing and handing me a shirt. Just a quick glance told me that this was a really fine shirt, and it must have a "name" label. Gucci, Chanel, Manhattan at Midnight and Camden Hills came to mind. I was not disappointed. There in the neck of the finely tailored blue-and-white-striped shirt was the information—L. L. Bean, Freeport, Maine. Even better than I had imagined! And the shirt was very nearly new. It was just great, a real find, but how could I paint in an L. L. Bean shirt? While considering this problem, I hastily handed over my 50 cents before the original owner or someone else would decide a mistake had been made and reclaim this treasure.

I decided that I would not actually paint in it. Spots of paint have a pretty final effect on most fabrics. But I could wear it for other activities and I could write in it. What author couldn't write better wearing a Bean shirt? The lillies of the field didn't earn their splendid colors; they were a token of God's grace. I didn't earn this appealing shirt, but here I was going home with it. Is it any wonder that I love rummage sales?

But I tell you that not even King Solomon with all his wealth had clothes as beautiful as one of these flowers.
                                                              Luke 12:27

Upstream

There is a pleasant stream to the north of my cabin. Its waters are cool and clear, coming down through the woodlands and past one or two small farmsteads. I have never been upstream very much myself, but here on a gravelly sand bar I find just one flaming scarlet poppy with tissue-thin petals, and I know that the seed floated down from the streamside yard of a lady who raises many beautiful flowers every year. Flotillas of oak leaves come drifting along. There are no oaks along my stretch of the stream, but upstream there must be strong sturdy oaks growing along the deep gulfs where the water flows. One time, two fat, placid Muscovy ducks floated down to see what was around the next bend, and then the next. And the little star-shaped cookie cutter that I often use was picked up along the water's edge.

And so it is that I catch glimpses of life in another place. There is beauty upstream, both domestic and wild. There is a sense of adventure and a longing to see a little life beyond the same familiar barnyard, and the person who sometimes loses things. Perhaps someday I will walk upstream and explore the other land that drops tokens of love and grace into the clear, rippling waters that pass close by my home. For the Creator has placed in all of us the desire to move upstream in our lives, toward Him and His dwelling place.

The Lord your God is bringing you into a fertile land—a land that has rivers and springs, and underground streams gushing out into the valleys and hills.
                                                       Deuteronomy 8:7

The Red Sea is Parting

On a sunny summer morning recently I was walking in the garden between the tomato rows and gave an involuntary scream as I almost stepped on a tomato hornworm that was crawling briskly along. Wherever it goes the tomato hornworm gets this general type of reaction (ugh!!).

However, before long the little monster will rearrange itself into the very beautiful hummingbird moth that hovers like a winged prayer at dusk before the midsummer garden flowers. I may never see the parting of the Red Sea, but isn't it nice to be able to step out almost any time and see some sort of miracle in the garden?

Moses held out his hand over the sea, and the Lord drove the sea back with a strong East wind. It blew all night and turned the sea into dry land. The water was divided, and the Israelites went through the sea on dry ground, with walls of water on both sides.

Exodus 14:21

Picking Okra Out of the Soup

For a few years when I was somewhat younger, I cleaned house once a week for the wife of my parish priest. My employer, who was a really fine gourmet cook, insisted on supplying me with a delicious lunch every cleaning day—no brown-bagging it on that job! I especially loved the homemade soups which my hostess often made. There were always little wheel-shaped bits of a vegetable in it that was unknown to me and that I especially liked. Faintly crunchy, tender, something like a very mild celery—I was told that this was okra.

My employer, whose roots were south and southwestern, told me that southern cooks never made soups, stews or pilaus without okra. She added, with an enigmatic smile, that her husband did not like okra and picked it all out of his soup. This explained why he studied the soups with such an absorbed intentness while spooning it up. I had always thought he was considering possible sermon topics or other ecclesiastical matters.

Since then I have found out a few more things about okra. Even though okra has a reputation as a southern vegetable, I discovered that the seed is sold by the Vermont Bean Seed Company, so it must grow in the north if the gardener is skillful enough. I also read in one of Hal Borland's books that his wife always grew it in their Connecticut garden but that Mr. Borland himself disliked it almost as much as he disliked rhubarb, which was quite a bit. He thought that if it was grown at all, it should be for the flowers, which he admitted are lovely. The dictionary revealed that okra originated in West Africa. And finally, in a gardening magazine, I came across an article called "Okra lovers, here's how to stretch your harvest." It was a fine little article slanted to okra people.

Apparently you either love okra, or you don't. There was a color photo of a blossoming okra plant. The blossom was a soft, delicate moth-like yellow. Okra would indeed be fine just as a flowering plant and then there would be the bonus of all those nice pods for soups and stews. I learned that the plants sometimes grow very tall, as "high as an elephant's eye," to quote the article. You can rejuvenate the plants by cutting them back to a height of about three feet and begin all over again, until the frosts come.

When discussing the subject with a friend recently her only comment was "But where did she get the okra?" This is a good question which I have not been able to solve as yet. I have been in some stores with very large produce departments lately but have not seen any okra, but it is out there somewhere, growing in gardens, mysterious, lovely, desirable.

What is the Kingdom of God like? What shall I compare it with? It is like this. A man takes a mustard seed and plants it in his field. The plant grows and becomes a tree, and the birds make their nests in its branches. Luke 13:18

On the War Path with Tecumseh

Now during the sweltering dog days of late July I go to the cool shadowed depths of the Great Gorge, looking for those lovely strange flowers, Indian Pipes. By careful searching I find several clumps of white ones and a lovely pink clump growing up through the leaf mulch beneath a giant hemlock. Each cool, translucent bloom is dusted with ashes, for they mark the place where some Indian warrior of long ago emptied out his pipe on the hunting grounds he loved. I think wistfully of the Indians who cherished the land that I love, too. It must have been hard for them to lose it.

I remember recently reading about Tecumseh, the great Shawnee Indian chief. He fell in love with a white woman, the daughter of pioneers in Illinois, and she taught him English, a knowledge of the Bible and Shakespeare. They would have married, but he could not leave his Indian life, and she could not adopt it for her own.

Tecumseh was a brilliant warrior with a fine mastery of all the ruses of forest warfare. One time he had laid siege to Fort Detroit, held by the British under General Hull. Hoping to convince Hull that thousands of warriors were lurking in the forest, Tecumseh marched his band of 600 Indians three times through a clearing in sight of the fort. Panic stricken, Hull surrendered without a shot being fired.

But gradually the Indians lost their beautiful land as, in a somewhat different way, we seem to be losing it today. Industrial complexes, housing and commercial developments of all kinds, nuclear plants with their dangerous wastes, wind-harnessing projects, pipelines, powerlines and roads are all edging relentlessly into both wild lands and farmlands. No place, however remote, is safe anymore. Plans are being made to build a great landfill on the lovely, isolated Tug Hill Plateau in my part of New York state. My own stream that I have loved so well for so many years has its headwaters there and will probably be polluted. Unless we can learn to deal with these problems conscientiously, and with innovative new methods, our lovely earth may gradually become uninhabitable.

Listen to my words, O Lord,
and hear my sighs.
Listen to my cry for help,
My God and king!
I pray to you O Lord;
you hear my voice in the
morning;
at sunrise I offer my prayers
and wait for your answer.

Psalm 5:1-3

Coming Out

Monarch butterflies flutter through the Bittersweet Garden all summer long, and the larvae, feeding on milkweed, are also often seen, but I never seem to find the chrysalids. However, this year in August I finally found one while weeding out the bayberry bushes. I had just yanked up a handful of old grass, and there, located on a dried out stalk only several inches from the basal end, was the little jade green urn, decorated with touches of black, as well as golden hobnails. The outline of the wings was visible through the glassy green sides. Not wishing to put it back on the ground where a meadow mouse might notice and nibble on it, I finally fastened with a clothes pin the strand of grass in a lilac bush just outside the kitchen window. It seemed that I hopefully would have a good view of the *coming out* from inside the house, and perhaps the changeling inside the lovely green casket would not remember that she had gone to sleep in a grass tangle and awakened in a lilac bush.

About nine days later, I observed that the chrysalid was darkening, first becoming bluish and then almost black, and now I could make out the orange and the black colors of the wings inside. The next day, about 10:30 in the morning, a rupture near the top of the chrysalid could be seen and about 11:45 the butterfly emerged. She clung to the empty chrysalid

19

and her wings looked like little wads of soft crumpled paper. She spent the first half-hour or so after emergence busily fitting the two parts of her proboscis together so that she will have an airtight tube for sucking nectar. She also climbed up a bit higher, to the clothes pin that had held her chrysalid in the bush, so that there would be room for her wings to hang down and gradually expand to their full size. By late afternoon the wings had been coaxed into shape and she was probably ready to fly, but the weather had become rainy, windy and cold. Very sensibly, she moved to the underside of a large lilac leaf and spent the night there.

At 8:30 the next morning I found her spreading her wings in the warm sunshine and before long she floated off through the air, landing on some Shasta daisies where she spent considerable time drinking nectar. Finally she flew off over the ridge pole of the house. The Shasta daisies had seemed to me to be rather shabby and drab this year and I had thought of moving them to a different location. But they had been fit for a queen (or a king) so I decided to leave them alone.

The butterfly will come to know the green meadows and all of the copses where the wildflowers grow, and especially that beloved delicacy, milkweed. When it came time for her to leave her enchanting little tomb, her bonds were loosened, her transformation was completed. Soon she was living a new life, unknown and unguessed at while she was a caterpillar tethered to a more terrestrial existence on a little plot of milkweed plants.

Just so, there was no way that the tomb could hold Jesus, and he is with us today in the sunlight and shadows of our lives.

"Take a guard," Pilate told them; "go and make the tomb as secure as you can."

Matthew 27:65

The Chickens Are Coming Home to Roost

One summer when I felt that not quite enough was going on around the homestead, I bought a flock of two-month-old Rhode Island Red chickens. They were sturdy little chickens that brightened up the hen room that had been empty for some time.

They awakened with the dawn and rushed to the doorway when I arrived with their feed. They fed with joy on the local feed store's best growing/laying mash and scratch feed, and welcomed handfuls of wild mustard and dandelion leaves, grass, and of course that special delight—chickweed. They also were happy to recycle bits of leftovers from the kitchen— crumbled bits of homemade bread, cottage cheese, apple parings and in fact almost anything edible. They loved to drink the fresh springwater that I carried to them and emptied into a cool earthenware crock.

They clucked and sang and shook out their feathers, and picked at my boots, and settled on their roosts at night with little sleepy murmurs of protest against the sun going down so soon. Before long they were repaying me for their care with lovely smooth, glossy brown eggs, retrieved from the straw-filled nests.

When the chickens were first purchased, a nearby neighbor called up every day or two to inquire if the chickens had been caught by anything (foxes, wild dogs, weasels, rats, skunks, coyotes) or had died of natural causes, which she seemed to think was very likely with chickens.

Finally, I announced firmly that I had made the hen house predator proof and that I had no intention of allowing them to be either caught or succumb to any ailments. I thought that my friend might have displayed a little more confidence both in the chickens and also their keeper.

And he said to them, "Why are ye so fearful? how is it that ye have no faith?"

Mark 4:40

21

A Hummingbird Summer

While walking along my old road on a hot June day I noticed a ruby-throated hummingbird flying about in some overhanging maple branches, catching small insects. Then it hovered over what appeared to be a small knot in a maple branch and finally settled down there. I suddenly realized that what seemed to be a knot in the wood was really the hummingbirds' nest, tiny and delicate, about the size of an eyecup.

Hummingbirds are familiar around my yard, but this was the first time I had ever seen one of their nests. Indeed, I had never really expected to, for the hummingbird is so elusive. There is Someone whose eye is on the sparrow and on the hummingbird, too, but for me it is a tricky business. After all, these are the little stunt flyers of the bird world. They not only can hover, and fly forward and backward, to the right or left, but they can also fly upside down!

I love a hummingbird summer, when it is a good year for these tiny bird folk who transact so much business with the flowers. It always seems lonesome, along about the middle of September, when suddenly one day I realize that the hummingbirds are gone. I sigh with a bit of loneliness as I think that even now *my* hummingbirds are perhaps flying nonstop the 575 perilous miles over the Gulf of Mexico to their winter home in Central America. Their tiny wings have to beat about 2,700,000 times on this part of the trip, over the open waters, that takes about 10 hours. Their small whirring wings may have to carry them through rain, fog, and wind. They must become very tired, but Someone keeps them on their course. My heart yearns over them and I know that God's heart does, too. May they arrive in safety, their way searched out for them by the same God who also wants to bring us to a safe journey's end.

Blessed is the man that heareth me, watching daily at my gates.

Prov. 8:34

News about the Blackberry Crop

The blackberry season seems to galvanize people into action who never bother picking any of the other wild berries. They disappear into the woods and return with milk pails full of plump, juicy berries, offering only meager information as to where they have been. Most generally they cautiously allow that the berries were "way back in" and "don't amount to much this year," perhaps adding that they found "just enough for a pie," with a discouraged vague expression on their faces that would do credit to a great, creative actor.

When blackberries are mentioned I can be just as sneaky as anyone else and am surprisingly vague about the location of favorite patches. A few standard phrases are solemnly used such as "they're all drying up," "the trees are crowding them out of the best places," or "I got lost the other day looking for some. Didn't think I'd ever make it out." This latter may be greeted with expressions of disbelief, for everyone is aware that I know this entire area, wild country and all, like the back of my hand.

But perhaps it is best for the blackberry picker to hunt up his own berries. Sometimes I think it is more fulfilling to find out things for ourselves, rather than always to depend on second-hand information. I think really good teaching is based on this premise. Anyway, it is a handy premise for the person who is trying to clutch blackberry treasure to his or her heart.

All living things look hopefully to you, and you give them food when they need it. You give them enough and satisfy the needs of all.

Psalm 145:15-16

Lost in the Woods

In an area southeast of my home there is a remote wild place of hills and deep ravines, heavily wooded with maple, beech, and lofty hemlocks, with small bubbling creeks and waterfalls. More than one neighbor has admitted to being lost in these hills.

One late summer's day I took a friend back into this beautiful wild section, home of the oven bird and the golden-winged warbler, beloved by all the shy, retiring forest folk. When we finally came to a breathtakingly deep ravine I suggested that we sit down and rest there in the hushed solemnity of the woods. But in an uneasy panic she insisted that we must go back and get out of the woods. So I took her out where we could look down upon meadows and farms and houses again. She told me that she had thought we were lost. "We weren't lost," I protested, "I knew where we were all the time." But she had been so stricken with fear that she had lost all confidence in my woods skills. Life can often be quite a disappointment to us in one way or another.

Jesus was often disappointed in his disciples. They did not seem to understand who he really was or what the kingdom of heaven was like. But one day when Jesus was praying alone, the disciples came to him and he asked them, "Who do people say the Son of Man is?" His disciples answered, "Some say John the Baptist. Others say Elijah, while others say Jeremiah or some other prophet." Then he asked the disciples "What about you? Who do you say I am?" and Peter answered, "You are the Messiah, the Son of the living God." In one glorious moment Peter finally understood who Jesus really was. May our eyes, too, be opened so that we see Jesus as our Savior, come to free us from our fears and failings and sins, to raise us to new life in his kingdom, which is all around us if we know where to look.

I assure you that whoever declares publicly that he belongs to me, the Son of Man will do the same for him before the angels of God.

Luke 12:8

Inspectors

Some friends of mine have a farm where they raise Belgian draft horses. A beautiful golden, honey-brown, they are often lined up against the pasture fence when I drive into the yard to make a visit. With lovely flowing manes and tails they are indeed handsome, whether at their country home or bedecked with rosettes of ribbons, taking prizes at horse shows or fairs.

Several months ago it was discovered with dismay that one of the horses had a severe injury to its leg, caused by getting tangled up in some wire fencing lying on the ground. It seems that the horse had pushed over the fence in the far end of the pasture and gone into a wooded, piney area. He had been doing this for some time, making trails and little cul-de-sacs where he stood browsing and enjoying the quiet solitude of the woods. But at last he caught his leg in the flattened wire and for many weeks his owners have been faithfully bandaging up the hurt area, and applying salves and ointments.

When I stopped in the other afternoon one of his care-givers was getting ready to tend to the bandaging. She was also grating up some carrots which she mixes with molasses and feeds to all of the horses along with their oats.

This horse got into trouble when he edged through his fence and went inspecting the earth. But he is being patiently cared for with love and skill. Horses that the prophet Zechariah saw in a vision were also out inspecting the earth. They found that the whole world was lying helpless and subdued. This sounds something like the world today. We need to love the earth with hope and perseverance, to respond by trying to heal its wounds, making it whole and beautiful again.

I saw an angel of the Lord riding a red horse. He had stopped among some myrtle trees in a valley, and behind him were other horses—red, dappled, and white. I asked him, "Sir, what do these horses mean?" He answered, "I will show you what they mean. The Lord sent them to go and inspect the earth."
Zechariah 1:8-11

Working in the Vineyard

Not long ago I asked a friend what her off-the-cuff thoughts were concerning the parable of the workers in the vineyard. "Oh," she sighed, "I've heard any number of sermons explaining this parable and I just don't know. Do *you* think someone can live all of their life hurting others, being cruel, selling drugs or whatever and then have a deathbed conversion and be forgiven everything?" Umm, well I don't really know. This is a tough one which is why I was asking my friend for an explanation instead of doing some mind-bending of my own on the subject.

There is of course, the main question, "Did the latecomers deserve as much pay as those who had worked all day in the vineyard?" Experience in our daily jobs seems to say, "Of course not." You check in on time or you will lose your job unless you've got a really innovative excuse. At least the men in the vineyard didn't make excuses. They simply said, "No one hired us." Nevertheless, they didn't appear to deserve nearly so much pay as the workers who were hired early in the day.

A few days after this discussion, I happened to be out by the side of my road at 4:30 in the afternoon of a dark, rainy day. The sun came out suddenly, misty droplets of rain sparkled, and in the eastern sky there appeared perhaps the most beautiful and complete rainbow I have ever seen. One end of the arch was hidden away in my beloved Folded Hills; the other was in the woods across the creek. I could look at it forever—the pale sulfur yellow, the strip of soft, mint green, the violet and pink. As I watched, two wild mallard ducks flew across it, quacking gently and carrying away rainbow drops on their wings.

I could not possibly leave the rainbow and get back to work, so I stayed and watched from the middle of the road where the view was unobstructed by trees. I wondered what I did to deserve seeing such a beautiful sight. I could so easily have been inside the cabin completely unaware of its presence.

The truth seems to be that I really didn't do anything special to deserve it, except perhaps to *be there*. But God in his great love allowed me to see, study and wonder about it. And I begin to feel that perhaps we are all really the latecomers to the vineyard with a continuing need to be redeemed by God's grace and love.

The kingdom of heaven is like this. Once there was a man who went out early in the morning to hire some men to work in his vineyard...

Matthew 20:1

Posted Signs

For various reasons youngsters do not seem to make really super berry-pickers. It was the hot blackberry moon of August when I took a small party of pickers to one of my favorite berry-picking haunts. An eleven-year-old who was among those present complained of: thirst, the sticky heat, bleeding bramble scratches, the need for a restroom, bees, hunger, and a scraped leg. Finally she said, "I don't like to pick on posted land." I replied firmly, "This land is never posted. Everyone comes here to pick," and went on vigorously detaching the delicious berries from the thorny canes. (I was attempting to provide a good industrious example to the subteenager.) "That looks like a posted sign to me," the child said, somewhat morosely. After straightening up my bent back with difficulty and taking an impatient look around, I discovered to my complete astonishment that she was right. On the maple tree around which we had been picking there was a brand new posted sign.

Well, as it says in St. Matthew's gospel, *Woe unto you, ye blind guides...*

Golden Glow

In my mind's eye I can still see this beautiful flower growing by the cellar hatchway of our Lake Ontario farm many years ago. I never heard of anyone planting golden glow—it was just *there* in the yard of the older homes. A hardy perennial with pale golden yellow double flowers, it began blooming in July and lasted until the hard frosts of autumn came.

The hatchway in our back yard led into the dim cool earthiness of the cellar, guarded by the golden glow flowers nodding in the soft summer winds. Nearby was a pear tree full of age and beauty that dropped its juicy ripe fruits into the grass, where they lay heavy and sun-warmed. Also close at hand was the smokehouse where my father cured hams and bacon he sold to summer people.

Those days have a dream-like quality about them now, and I have never seen golden glow since we left that farm. It does not seem to be in the seed catalogs. An occasional trimming of the surrounding grass with a scythe was about the only care it needed, so it was a good flower for a busy farm. And the blooms came when many other flowers were dried up and gone in the heat of late summer. We picked the bright flowers for kitchen table bouquets and to take to our little country cemetery.

Every life has its shadow and hurts, but then God gives us signs of his enduring love, like beautiful, dependable *golden glow.*

> *And now the light in the sky is dazzling,*
> *Too bright for us to look at it;*
> *and the sky has been swept*
> *clean by the wind.*
> *A golden glow is seen in the north*
> *and the glory of God fills us*
> *with awe.*

Job 37:21-22

Elderberry Pie

Elderberry pies have always been just about the favorite kind of pie in my family. As a result, the number one priority wherever we have lived is to locate a good source of the berries. This is not always easy. Many birds also love these fruits that are so beautiful, with a high vitamin C content, and they may strip the bushes, while other less astute pickers are still only dreaming about elderberries. So, if possible it is best to locate a place where they grow in profusion so that there will really be enough of a harvest to go around.

The elderberry blooms in late June when the early spring flowers are gone. Each little elderberry floret looks as if it had been fashioned from heavy white silken cloth. There is a great drift of them in a damp swale near the cabin.

When it is time to make elderberry pie, I will be using a recipe given to me by a church friend, a gracious, kind-hearted lady and an exceptionally fine cook. She says the sour cream cuts the musky flavor of the berries a bit. I know it makes a great pie for I have eaten:

Mary's Elderberry Pie

> About 3 cups elderberries
> ½ cup light brown sugar
> ½ cup white sugar
> dash salt
> 1½ tablespoons minute tapioca
> 2-3 tablespoons commercial sour cream

Mix all together and let set while fixing pie crust (makes 9" pie). Put one tablespoon cut-up butter or margarine on top of pie crust. Bake at 400 degrees about 10 minutes and then 350 degrees for 30 to 40 minutes.

A sensible man gathers the crops when they are ready; it is a disgrace to sleep through the time of harvest.(!)

Proverbs 10:5

Substitutions

Many years ago my uncle served as a caretaker on the estate of people who had inherited one of the great cereal fortunes of America. When I was about eight years old my family visited him at this estate and one of the wonders my uncle showed us was an artificial brook that rippled along as naturally as if it had always been there.

I was fascinated and, back home, I tried to create just such a brook in an old cement floored cellarhole that was on our farm. I borrowed wash tubs and cooking pots from my mother and trowels and shovels from my father and pumped up endless pails of fresh well-water, but with all my efforts I could not produce a flowing stream.

Only God can create real springs of living water that runs through the valleys and makes our lives pleasant and even possible. Indeed, only God is able to create and sustain a habitable earth with all its variety of plant life and creatures both great and small. Now the twilight of life has come to many of his marvellous creations. The condor, the peregrine falcon, the bald eagle, the wolves, possibly even the bluebirds have an uncertain hold on life.

We need to ask God to help us to walk more gently on this earth and to care for it with skill and love. The difficulties are grave, but what could we ever find to substitute for the flight of a hummingbird, the cool shade of maple trees, the wind murmuring through golden aspen leaves? The stately beauty of a wild meadow lily or the glowing vibrant colors of a Polyphemus moth?

I will make rivers flow among barren hills and springs of water run in the valleys.

Isaiah 41:18

Fishing Holes

As I walk along the creek this morning, Kingfisher, bright and sharp as usual in his union-blue outfit, goes rattling noisily past me. He eyes me blandly, almost with amusement, I fancy. Probably he knows that I have wandered along this creek for almost 30 years now and have never yet located a Kingfisher's nest.

However, my time has not been wasted. I have watched in amazement as Kingfisher dived head first into shadowy pools beneath the willow trees. It would seem that he must surely end up with a severe concussion, but no, he emerges triumphantly holding a minnow and rattles on upstream—not quite so loudly now, for the same reason that we can only speak in muffled tones when our mouth is full.

I have found the one place where Spiranthes lucida, a tiny delicate white northern orchid, grows. It is one of the Ladies' Tresses. The thick beds of spearmint, that I use for my spearmint jelly, yielded up the secrets of their whereabouts to me. And I learned where swift deep water flows fast through narrow rocky channels, just perfect for washing clothes or hair. I learned a lot of things, but not where the Kingfishers raise their top-knotted babies.

One time I asked an old-time fisherman if he had ever known the location of a Kingfishers' nest. "Oh, sure," he replied, eyeing me pityingly, "Used to nest for years over near a bridge on North Sandy. Albinos—all white!" "White!" I exclaimed, "I never heard of an albino Kingfisher. Are you sure they were Kingfishers?" "Oh sure—do a lot of damage in a fishing stream," he added, looking at me severely, as if he thought I might be responsible for Kingfishers. Well, I'm not, but Someone is, and I am glad, for they brighten up any stream or river with their interesting lifestyle.

Every autumn it seems lonesome when Kingfisher abandons my stream for his southern haunts. And in the spring it always seems that life is picking up again when I hear him noisily gargling his way upstream and then down, probably checking to see if his favorite fishing holes are still intact.

Wherever the stream flows there will be all kinds of animals and fish. The stream will make the water of the Dead Sea fresh, and wherever it flows, it will bring life.

Ezekiel 47:9

Lessons from a Beaver Pond

One day during the changing leaf moon of autumn some friends drove me in to see the beaver pond, using their four-wheel-drive pickup. It was a lovely drive with only one passage that seemed rather unsettling to me. This was the place where the road passed over a very old iron bridge spanning a ravine that was quite breathtakingly deep.

The pond seemed vast and perhaps was once an alder swamp as many alders grew in the flooded area, appearing unharmed by the higher water level. The water was quite silty. I imagine autumn is an especially busy time for the beaver— building up their underwater food pile, tightening up the dam, working on the spillways and canals; and no doubt the pond sediment gets stirred up more than usual.

One spillway was near the road and I could see beaver paw and tail marks there in the slick mud. Off to one side was a canal leading to a grove of poplar trees, a favorite beaver food. There was a felled poplar tree, its yellow leaves still shaking in the breeze as if in remembrance of its former upright position. A few buttery yellow "beaver lilies" floated on the water. And a maple tree, its leaves a flaming red, decorated a little rocky point on the southern side of the pond.

Beaver are quiet, mostly nocturnal animals, and we heard no beaver sounds. There were just the gentle murmuring noises of the wind and the water. One splashing noise, a

33

little louder, might have been a beaver's tail striking the water, at the far edge of the pond.

But I felt a tremendous sense of expectancy as I looked at the beaver pond. I knew instinctively that the pond was a place of life, of abundant life. The beaver were there, watching over their pond, perhaps resting a bit somewhere along the banks, or plastering their lodge with some fresh mud or deepening the tunnels to the lodge, happy in their well-flooded kingdom. I was reminded of the book of Genesis—"and the power of God was moving over the water."

The beaver pond experience seemed to me something like prayer; we do not pray with a feeling of emptiness and futility, the feeling that I get when I have been talking on the telephone, only to discover I have been put on hold and no one is hearing me. We pray with a deep conviction that God is there, listening to us, knowing us, loving us.

He let you hear his voice from heaven so that he could instruct you; and here on earth he let you see his holy fire, and he spoke to you from it.

Deuteronomy 4:36

Line Storm

I asked a friend to look over a manuscript concerning a lost homing pigeon. In the original copy I had referred to an autumn storm as a "line storm." My friend exclaimed, "Line storm! But what is a line storm?"

It had never occurred to me that anyone might not know what a line storm was. I thought of my years growing up on a farm. There would come a day in late September when the fall rains began, slanting down in wind-blown sheets against the windows, and branches fell from the huge willow tree in the yard. The cows forlornly huddled around the watering tank in the barnyard, only too glad to be driven back into the barn again. And my father, coming to the house for dinner, rain dripping from coat, cap and boots into puddles on the floor, gasped, "Line storm," trying to get his breath again after a losing battle with the elements.

I never was able to explain a line storm very well to my friend. I hesitantly went on about the celestial equator, the sun crossing a line ("What line? A celestial equator, what is that? And why would that cause a storm?") Finally, giving up, I admitted that I would need to do some studying to really explain a line storm. I did the studying and still don't really understand it; I never did get very good marks in school on that little matter of the orange traveling around the sun. I even began to wonder if there was such a thing as a line storm anymore.

I asked my country friend who finds God while trout fishing if he remembered the old-fashioned line storm. "Oh sure," he said matter-of-factly, and went on to explain how such a storm came about, losing me almost at once. "Well," I finally asked, "Is there also one in the spring?" (I don't seem to remember so much about line storms in the spring of the year.) "Oh sure," he said, "Old timers used to call it the 'lilac storm.' Usually comes when the lilacs are out."

This left me completely confused, as lilacs, around here anyway, come out in May and the equinox is in March. Well, anyway, lilac storm has a lovely sound to it. I am sure a lilac storm would be something special. And just to be on the safe side, I didn't refer to the storm in the pigeon meditation as a line storm.

The one thing I positively remember from an old-time line storm was that when you were in the midst of one you knew it. As we know surely that it is Jesus when he speaks to us. As Mary Magdalene knew him when he spoke to her in the garden after the crucifixion.

Jesus said to her "Mary!" She turned toward him and said in Hebrew, "Rabboni!"

John 20:16

35

Stemming Elderberries

This is the busy harvest season when storage space must be found for the beans and pumpkins and squash that the well-tended garden has produced, sometimes in overwhelming abundance. There are also some very tempting wild crops to be garnered. This reminds me of a young neighborhood farmer whose favorite pie is elderberry.

Earlier this fall he picked two bushel baskets full of the huge flat clusters of berries, and with pride took them home to his mother. She viewed his treasure and then announced succinctly, although perhaps somewhat ungrammatically, that "if you want a pie, you can stem them berries yourself."

I know through my own experience that it can be hard to stop picking elderberries. The stems of the clusters are brittle and break off easily, and one reaches ever higher in the bushes, toward the blue autumn sky, to get just one more cluster so it won't be "wasted on the birds." But afterwards, when the excitement of picking is over, it is very tedious work to rake off the small berries by hand.

My sister-in-law has solved this problem in quite an adroit fashion. She often needs to make farm-connected trips to feed stores, implement dealers and so forth and when asked to go on one of these errands she puts a pail of elderberries in the truck. Then while she is waiting (and a farm wife logs a lot of time just waiting) she can pick off elderberries, which seems like an astonishingly practical method of using spare time, and keeping ahead of the elderberry pickers.

As long as the world exists, there will be a time for planting and a time for harvest. There will always be cold and heat, summer and winter, day and night.

Genesis 8:22

Mail Order Churn

As I reflect about my move from the big eleven-plus-room farmhouse to the little twelve by twenty-four foot cabin, I think how well it turned out after all, even though at the time it seemed impossible. Friends in West Virginia inquired if I had been able to find room for my dog and two cats. I wrote back that they "went in first and that everything else was worked in around them."

I had to let some long-cherished heirlooms be sold in the household auction just before moving day but I managed to bring with me many smaller treasured items, even including the little Sears Roebuck electric churn that mother bought from the mail order company in the early forties. The metal part is a nice, soft, pale green with two wooden hinged lids on top and clean wooden paddles within. It served us well during a time when farming conditions were unsettled and milk strikes were often called.

First a used milk separator was located and then the churn was purchased. No longer was it a catastrophe when unsold milk overflowed every available container, for the milk could be made into butter both for our own use and to be sold to summer people along the lake shore, and other customers who liked "homemade" butter better than "store-bought."

The butter for our own table was always placed in an antique white ironstone dish that everyone in our family considered to be a butter dish. We were told once or twice by purists, however, that this was really a soap dish. It did not matter to us—it still seemed as fine as the one mentioned in the biblical Song of Deborah—"She brought forth butter in a lordly dish."

My very first memory of churning dates back to 1936. There had been a three-day blizzard closing the roads, and my father had been unable to take any cream to the creamery for quite a few days. The cream was fast accumulating, so my father took the horses and sleigh and went to my grandparents' home to borrow their churn. The churn was the old-fashioned barrel kind, set on a sturdy framework and turned by hand with a crank. Just getting it transported to our little snowbound farmhouse was quite a problem. Grandmother, muffled up in heavy clothing, came along with it; she did not think my parents knew enough about making butter to manage on their own.

It was an exciting day with many difficulties. Even the water pump had frozen up and had to be thawed out with tea kettles full of hot water before the churning could start. But it all turned out well. Under grandmother's kindly supervision enough fresh butter was made to last us for the rest of the winter.

Meanwhile, here at my cabin, the little mail-order churn is a symbol of faith to me. Faith that, whether churning butter or moving into a new home, life is never impossible when He is with us.

When you pass through deep waters, I will be with you.
                                                                Isaiah 43:2

Going Home

Jesus tried to make clear to his followers that he came not as earthly rulers do, desiring power and wealth, but as a servant to the least of these our brothers. This was not easy for the disciples to understand and on at least one occasion they fell into an argument as to which of them should be thought of as the greatest.

It is not easy for us today to serve our Lord with quiet humility, seeking only to do his will and not concerning ourselves with our own advancement. We even wonder sometimes if God does really need us. After all, there are so many highly talented, competent people in the world. However, there is always something that each one of us can do that no one else is in a position to do.

This is the way it was on a stormy day in the fall when I found a homing pigeon resting on my back porch. The bird seemed stunned and exhausted, beaten down by the winds and rain and hail.

An empty bird cage had been in the farmhouse when we came there in 1959 and had never been thrown away, as "it might come in handy someday." I placed the pigeon inside, with dishes of grain and water and set the cage in a quiet, safe corner of the summer kitchen. After several days the pigeon seemed rested and alert again and one morning I found it quietly standing in the cage facing hopefully toward the south. Since the weather was now sunny and warm, I took the cage outside, opening the door, and the pigeon flew out and upward. In a flurry of beautiful beating wings it oriented itself to the sun, the wind, the trees, and everything else that is meaningful to a homing pigeon and soon it was flying steadily southward. I knew that perhaps hundreds of miles away was its beloved home and some anxious owner would be watching the skies for the first sight of his beautiful racing bird come home at last.

But I am among you as one who serves.

Luke 22:27

Meeting at the Apple Trees

Friends of mine have a tree farm in quite a remote place back in the hills. It started out as a Christmas tree farm but somehow the trees (pine, spruce and balsam), so tiny when set out, stretched upward in no time at all and suddenly were much too large for Christmas trees. My friends spent a lot of their spare time pruning, and thinning their trees, working up firewood and "swamping out" woods roads. Now the owners just say mysteriously that the trees are an investment for the grandchildren.

They have a little cabin there and also what is delicately referred to as a "convenience." For some reason porcupines zeroed in on the "convenience," demolishing large chunks of

39

the outer siding of plywood and particle board. They left big, ragged holes that had to be covered with more plywood if privacy was to be maintained within. This work was done amid threats of violence to Porcupine if caught.

While visiting in early April I checked to see how the "convenience" wintered-over. I discovered that it had not fared too well. Much of the interior had been demolished, leaving the "throne" in quite a precarious condition. A lovely tiny quill gave a clue as to the identity of the guilty party. There must be glues, resins or something in this man-made lumber that is especially appealing to Porcupine. I can see how his nonchalant assault on this last bastion of privacy could be maddening to a non-porcupine person.

But I can think of last autumn when I was resting in the woods' edge after picking up a basket of windfall apples. The leaves were enchanting shades of gold and scarlet and yolk yellow, the sky was a deep, bright blue. It was a lovely day, but the breezes sighed through the uncut meadow grasses and it seemed a little lonesome until I heard a preoccupied, sing-song murmuring noise, and there up in an apple tree was Porcupine. He looked down at me with bright, dark eyes and seemed to think I was harmless, for he just continued feeding on a lovely, rosy red apple freckled with gold, turning it about in his forepaws, chewing down into the juicy goodness of autumn's bounty.

It no longer seemed lonesome. Here was pleasant, interesting company, sharing the earth with me on this wistful, dreaming day of autumn. And perhaps this phlegmatic little fellow, who generally is the object of a good many vituperative comments, was happy for my uncritical, loving companionship. In our own way, we each savored God's beautiful season of glowing autumn.

Then God commanded, "Let the earth produce all kinds of animal life: domestic and wild, large and small"—and it was done. So God made them all, and he was pleased with what he saw.   Genesis 1:24

Puzzles

Recently I was in a store where I noticed some very large stacks of picture puzzles in the center of one of the aisles. This seemed like a good opportunity to buy a Christmas present for a friend who loves putting puzzles together. So I knelt down and started searching through the pile for the perfect picture for my friend.

Suddenly, much to my embarrassment, the immense assortment of puzzles began sliding down around me and out into the aisle, and my position was such that if I moved at all the rest of the pile was going to tumble down in the same manner, something like an avalanche on Mt. Washington.

Busy friends, neighbors, acquaintances, even store personnel that I had known for years simply detoured around or stepped over the puzzles and myself without even a glance or a word of encouragement. Possibly they thought I was trying to think of my mantra or was putting on a protest demonstration of some sort. Anyway it suddenly occurred to me that this *was* the parable of the Good Samaritan. It was exciting to realize that one was involved in a real parable and that the Good Samaritan must be somewhere in this anxious, hurried crowd of Halloween shoppers.

Sure enough, an elderly, white-haired lady with a merry twinkle in her eye stopped and asked, "My dear, can I help you?" "Oh," I sighed in relief, "I would love some help." And so, with the aid of this kindly lady the puzzles were restacked and order was restored. The lady had some good advice too. She said not to buy a puzzle with too much autumn foliage as they were especially hard to put together. I breathed a prayer of thanks for this lady who had grown in kindliness and wisdom and joy through the years so that she did not mind getting "involved" to help someone in trouble.

But the teacher of the Law wanted to justify himself, so he asked Jesus, "Who is my neighbor?"

Luke 10:29

Licorice Sticks and Martyrs

I have always had a great deal of admiration for the old timers who sturdily ate such things as eel soup, head cheese, hasty pudding and licorice candy. In fact, anyone with the strength of character to enjoy licorice candy is held in amazed esteem, no matter what type of body their spirit is dwelling in.

So it is that while brooding over a mouse problem that seems to be quite widespread this fall, I have noticed that every evening, about 8:00, a deer mouse, all fawn golden and white, with huge dark eyes, whiskers his way to the top of a bookcase, and nibbles a bit on some black licorice sticks, left there in a long-forgotten housekeeping upheaval. Then he vanishes for the night. This reminds me that saints and sages, heroes, prophets and martyrs can be found in quiet, small, unexpected places, sometimes quite obscure and unapplauded.

But when she could not hide him any longer, she took a basket made of reeds and covered it with tar to make it watertight. She put the baby in it and then placed it in the tall grass at the edge of the river.

Exodus 2:3

A Penguin for the Christmas Tree

According to his own account, the prophet Isaiah was a sinful man living among sinful people, but even so he was given a vision of God. So, too, we often fall short of what we might be, but we also sometimes have moments when we know God has allowed us to see or feel or know or do something special.

Last Advent I was in a gift shop where I happened to find a box of little carved wooden Christmas tree ornaments made from Stony Point red cedar. As I touched the beautiful aromatic wood I remembered growing up on a Stony Point farm, the shoreline washed by the waves of Lake Ontario. I could see again the red cedars with their misty blue berries that covered much of the inland area. I remembered the good times and the hard times (for those were Depression and then later war years) that our family had.

I bought a little penguin for my Christmas tree, a token of a life long gone, but remembered with joy and sometimes regret. So God gives us these small poignant memories of our lives, and always we hope to build on the foundation of our previous days a life ever more holy, good and acceptable in his sight.

. . .And yet with my own eyes I have seen the King, the Lord Almighty.

Isaiah 6:5

David's Royal Line

Sometimes in Europe the top growth of trees such as willows is cut back by wood cutters so that new shoots will grow out from the trunk. In this country one usually sees it only occasionally, but there is a willow along my creek that was cracked off by ice jams several years ago. Now the broken stump is bristling with new shoots and there is a little, protected room in the center where Muskrat often sits and browses on whatever forage he has found, holding cattail shoots or willow stems or apples in his knobby little fists. In summer he is shaded by the flickering gold-green willow leaves. In late fall his accomodations are barer and more austere. His spirit is somewhat remote and withdrawn as he rests on his safe platform above the dark, swirling waters, perhaps browsing on a bit of sweet flag root.

Isaiah uses the image of a tree cut down but sprouting

new branches from the stump to foretell the coming of a new king from among the descendants of David. As we make our way through Advent we try to learn how best to welcome this new king among us and make Him glad that He has come.

The royal line of David is like a tree that has been cut down; but just as new branches sprout from a stump, so a new king will arise from David's descendants.

Isaiah 11:1

The Star on the Top of the Tree

Usually, in early December I set out with a saw and an axe, accompanied by my collie dog who loves any kind of an outdoor expedition, and cut down a small spruce or pine tree from an area of reforestation not far away. Back home again I decorate it with garlands of popcorn and cranberries, tinsel, tiny salt-dough Christmas ornaments, other small ornaments bought mostly at craft fairs, and colored balls that were used on our family Christmas trees of long ago.

For the star on the very top of the tree I use an antique tin maple sugar mold in the shape of a star. It is a little dented around the edges but it has the lovely dim glow of old tin and really looks nice up in the fragrant evergreen branches. And its dentedness reminds me of our lives that seem always to get a little dented around the edges in this life. But then our Savior comes to us at Christmas time and we live again whole and complete in his all-encompassing love that makes all things new, and mends the broken-hearted.

God did not choose us to suffer his anger, but to possess salvation through our Lord Jesus Christ, who died for us in order that we might live together with him, whether we are alive or dead when he comes.

1 Thess. 5:9-10

Coyotes

Dusk comes early in December and as I walk toward the woodshed after a final check on the hen house I hear the coyotes calling back in the hills. Their song rises and falls, wailing and sobbing and sighing. As the northern lights seem like a luminous veil of light ever diminishing and then flashing out over the sky in endless fascination, so does the call of even one coyote throb and sing like a thousand wild violins (or coyotes). I am glad they are safe for tonight back in the hills, protected by the deep snow from the dangers that are always the lot of the coyote, or little wild running brush dog.

So we too rejoice when we are safe. Only when we are safe in His love can we venture forth to take risks and chances for His sake. Then we can risk humiliation when we apologize for the unthinking words we have said, risk loss of social standing when we befriend someone who is not quite up to the standards of our group, whether it be conduct, dress or economic viability; whatever the risk is of upsetting our comfortable routine, we are willing to take it for His sake.

But all who find safety in you will rejoice, they can always sing for joy.

Psalm 5:11

Other Worlds

John the Baptist's mission was to preach and baptize with water, preparing the people for the coming of Jesus who would be greater than he and would baptize with the Holy Spirit.

Advent is a time when we, too, prepare for the coming of Jesus. Recently I followed a fox trail through the snow and eventually entered a lovely, small world I would never have noticed if I had not been tracking the fox. It was a very low-ceilinged area, barely a foot high, beneath the spreading

branches of a large copse of spruces. It was densely carpeted with fallen golden-brown spruce needles and tiny dried forest flowers, protected from wind and cold by the thick low-sweeping branches covered with insulating snow. The fox apparently spent cold, stormy days lying here with his nose tucked into his fluffy tail, warm and secure through the dreariest weather.

This is the kind of room we need to prepare in our hearts for the coming of Jesus—a lovely room where he can enter in and be with us no matter how dismal the weather is outside. A place where he is always welcome and where the fragrance of evergreen reminds us that our redeemer has come to live with us and bring us everlasting life and joy and peace.

God said, "I will send my messenger ahead of you to open the way for you. Someone is shouting in the desert, 'Get the road ready for the Lord; make a straight path for him to travel!'"

Mark 1:2-3

Waiting

Back in the days when gasoline was fairly cheap, our family sometimes occupied ourselves pleasantly on a Sunday afternoon by "taking a ride." We often drove to an area that had many interesting abandoned roads. This had once been a farming section, but the soil was not too deep and the growing season quite short so it was gradually reverting to woods.

In so many of the little houses we passed, no matter how tumbledown or unpainted, we would see spectacular geraniums in the windows or small glassed-in porches. I think in the years since then I have never seen such geraniums, in particular the beautiful deep-glowing reds and now and then an especial treasure, the Martha Washington geranium. They were always growing in old tin cans that had once held tomatoes or corn or fruit. No fancy plastic or clay containers or complicated soil mixes, but the plants flourished amazingly, filling the windows with bright color.

In a way, the memory of these lovely plants reminds me of the ministry of Jesus. He never had an easy time bringing his message of love and redemption to God's people, always surrounded by opposition and disbelief. Even John, who had baptized Jesus in the Jordan river, began to have some gloomy doubts about him. While John was confined in a prison cell he sent his own disciples to question Jesus. "Tell us," they asked Jesus, "Are you the one John said was going to come, or should we expect someone else?" Jesus told the disciples "Go back and tell John what you are hearing and seeing: the blind can see, the lame can walk, those who suffer from dreaded skin diseases are made clean, the deaf hear, the dead are brought back to life and the Good News is preached to the poor. How happy are those who have no doubts about me!"

". . . The words that I have spoken to you," Jesus said to his disciples, "do not come from me. The Father, who remains in me, does his own work."

John 14:10

Finding Time

I do not exactly live on the cutting edge of our high-tech culture. Nevertheless, I have become aware that there is a new kind of television called digital television. One advantage of this new development is that you can watch more than one program at a time on a split screen. This seems to be a fine idea, for it brings television more in line with real life where, from the time of Martha in the Bible down to the present, we are often overly busy and troubled with many things all at the same time. Especially around Christmas we are likely to fret about our inability to get everything done on time—the cards, the presents, the fruitcakes, the trees and decorations, the Christmas dinner and so on.

Although I usually take things more calmly, still I was having quite a hectic time one December evening. While threading a popcorn chain for the tree I stabbed the needle into my hand, necessitating some first-aid work with a bottle of iodine. At the same time a strange crashing, dragging noise could be heard in the woodshed. Investigation revealed that an opossum had come through a door that had been accidentally left open, and had tripped over a basket containing ears of popcorn. He was wringing his small pink hands dolefully as the tiny, hard, sharp kernels of popcorn didn't seem very pleasing to him after all. He was also making low unfriendly growling noises at the cat. After removing the cat, I found a sweet, yellow, windfall apple for the opossum, and then had to rush inside to answer the telephone. A lady was calling from a TV rating organization to find out what I was watching. She was really surprised to hear that there was no television in my house.

After everything quieted down I went back to decorating the tree, glad that there was finally time to find especially good places among the fragrant evergreen boughs for the tiny blue and white Virgin Mary, the stained glass angel, the little celluloid Santa Claus from Christmas trees of other years—and glad that God had not been too busy to prepare for that first Christmas Eve in Bethlehem.

There were some shepherds in that part of the country who were spending the night in the fields taking care of their flocks. An angel of the Lord appeared to them, and the glory of the Lord shone over them. They were terribly afraid, but the angel said to them "Don't be afraid. I am here with good news for you, which will bring great joy to all the people."

Luke 2:8-10

Helping Out

As the Christmas season approaches, I have been remembering a December some years ago when I lived on a farm near Belleville. Each day seemed to be stormier and colder and bleaker than the day before. About the twenty-third a kindly lady in the neighborhood, who was always the first to know when anyone was in trouble, called up to say that she was sorry to bother us right at Christmas time but that an elderly man who lived alone was all out of food and fuel and even his chickens had hardly anything left to eat. She was asking all the neighbors to bring in supplies to keep him going until permanent assistance could be arranged.

Mother and I responded to this emergency by getting together a box of staple foods, as well as canned foods and casserole dishes, and I filled a sack with corn and wheat for the chickens and we set off in the car over some badly drifted roads to the small country house where the man lived.

I had a picture in my mind of a gentle, stooped old man with silvery hair and perhaps a shawl over his shoulders, who would lay a frail hand on my arm and in a quavering voice express his thanks to us for coming out on such a terrible winter's day to assist him. Perhaps his house would need some sweeping and dusting and straightening up while the old man sat in a rocker by the fire looking grateful.

The old man, however, turned out not to be stooped and gray at all, or especially gentle either. Actually he looked like a pirate, with a merry, outrageous twinkle in his eye, hair that was still almost completely black, and a spine that was as straight as a ruler. One could almost see him stomping around on a quarterdeck, forcing reluctant foes to walk the plank and luring captured ladies into trouble with his wild, mirthful ways. Although his house was pretty bare, it was so clean it looked as though he swabbed the whole place down every day with buckets of water to the accompaniment of wild sailor chanteys. Actually, this was not altogether a fanciful idea; he had been a sailor on the Great Lakes during his working years.

On the way home I gloomily complained to mother that the object of our charity looked like a pirate. "Well," mother pointed out, "maybe he did look different than what we were expecting, but he was in need. There wasn't a thing to eat in that kitchen except what neighbors have started bringing in. That barrel where he kept his chicken feed was empty, wasn't it?"

Looking back over the years I can see that this was true. After all, Jesus did not set many guidelines for our responses to need, to hunger, to loneliness, and fear and despair. He simply said, "Whenever you did this for one of the least important of these brothers of mine, you did it for me."

The righteous will then answer him, "When, Lord, did we ever see you hungry and feed you, or thirsty and give you a drink?"
Matthew 25:37

The King is Coming

When we prepare to greet this king at Christmas time we do not need to keep our distance if we are lowly and poor, either in body or spirit. One Christmas when I was a child during the Great Depression, my father, who was a poor struggling farmer then, had only $1.89 to spend for gifts. He spent it all for oranges, partly because we all loved them and partly because they reminded him of his own boyhood when there was always an orange in the toe of the stocking. He fashioned a homemade baseball bat out of a sturdy piece of ashwood for my two brothers and somehow my mother managed to make a passable catcher's mitt to go with the bat. She made new doll clothes for my favorite doll and tiny maple sugar cakes for all of us. It certainly was a simple Christmas but we all were very happy and thought that no one else had quite such a good Christmas as we did.

I have sometimes felt that we make our Christmases too complicated, perhaps spending excessively for gifts when small, carefully selected, or homemade, tokens of our love would be just as acceptable. We get involved in more busy activities than we can really handle when, after all, the best thing we can do is to simply join the shepherds as they "go to Bethlehem to see this thing that has happened, which the Lord has told us."

Over the years, I have sometimes told the story of my father and the oranges. I remember one year I was telling this story to my priest's wife (the one who introduced me to okra). Apparently I had told it to her several times before because just as I got nicely started she hastily forestalled me; with a thoughtful smile she said, "I always love that part about the oranges!"

Anyway, I still like to remember that year when there were plenty of oranges and a great deal of love but not too much else. Not a bad way at all to celebrate the coming of a baby to a humble stable in Bethlehem.

The Lord God will make him a king, as his ancestor David was, and he will be the king of the descendants of Jacob forever; his kingdom will never end.

Luke 1:32-33

Stables

Recently I was in the small barn of a friend who raises sheep. It was cold and bleak outside but the warmth of the sheep made it seem very pleasant inside. They were pulling down delicate wisps of sweet-smelling clover and timothy hay from mangers built out of poplar boards along one side of the barn. A row of windows on the south side let in what sunshine there was on this short December day. Cakes of beet pulp were laid out for the sheep and clean straw was under foot.

A jersey cow that gives milk for the family was tied at one side of the barn and quietly mooed as we petted her. Here in the stable with the gentle herdswoman, always attentive to the needs of her animals, I thought of the birth of Jesus. It would have been hard to love a Savior born in a palace or a fine inn as much as we are able to love Jesus, who was born in a stable. A stable can be a wonderful place indeed. Especially at this time of year it is a welcome refuge from the storms and cold of the outdoors, a place where new life comes into being and where new hope is stirred up for the farm person.

She gave birth to her first son, wrapped him in cloths and laid him in a manger—there was no room for them to stay in the inn.

Luke 2:7

A Living Psalm

"You know," a neighbor told me, "deer are dumb the way they yard-up in winter." I looked my astonishment. "Deer dumb?" My friends, the deer, who tuck their fawns away in the wild apple orchard, who muzzle down and find the sweetest beechnuts on the ridge in autumn, who once sneaked away from my view by crouching down and crawling through a barbed wire fence?

They are God's cattle on thousands of hills. And how about the little gray screech owl that on very stormy days sometimes perches on a little ledge above a sheltered window where he looks very wise and small, and is a constant outrage to the blue jays who shout their scandalized protests, and the snowshoe hare with the big forest dark eyes and outsize feet who sleeps beneath the back stoop in the daytime. These all belong to God. And so as the psalmist says, all the earth and its inhabitants belong to God and he does not need our sacrifices and burnt offerings. Instead, the giving of thanks should be our sacrifice to God—thanksgiving for our lives, for the special abilities that each one of us has, for giving us the means to grow in his grace and love.

All the animals in the forest are mine and the cattle on thousands of hills. All the wild birds are mine and all living things in the fields.

Psalm 50:10-11

Pheasants

Last summer some hunters stocked the area around the farm with young pheasants, even though they seldom seem to survive the severe winters here. Through the autumn I sometimes heard the startling squawk of a male pheasant coming from a small nearby swale where flickering willow leaves were turning to a rusty, freckled gold. Or sometimes from the edge of the pine plantation where they roosted at night. One fall day when a carload of hunters drove by on the old road they asked me if I had seen any pheasants around and I courteously assured them that I had not. I added, with a puzzled air, that I couldn't think where they had all gone to. Even while I was bidding the hunters farewell, I thought of the beautiful, colorful pheasant who was lurking behind a nearby straw stack. Which was a nice safe place for him to be while the hunters blasted away now and then far down the abandoned road.

The pheasants made the autumn a more special season than ever, but with a touch of melancholy, too. For, lovely as this hushed, waiting season is with dreaming Indian summer days, there is always the knowledge that one day soon all this will change to a time of bitter, penetrating cold. I felt sure that for the pheasants life would slowly, perhaps painfully, fade away.

As the Beaver Moon advanced, a few of the introduced birds were lost to hunters and some were caught by foxes, coyotes and other predators. Then the hard winter set in. Day after day winds scoured the earth and harsh sleet storms coated the fields with ice. I began to see just two handsome cock pheasants out in the threadbare fencerows and fields, struggling to find food beneath the ice and snow. I tried putting out corn for them but at first they did not find it, the world was such a large, bleak place. Finally, after Christmas, I made a little bower out of brush and some thick pine branches on the edge of the back yard. Beneath the brush pile I laid an old barrel on its side and spread corn and wheat inside the barrel. A nearby woodpile served as a windbreak and so this project made a protected, appealling place for the pheasants if only they could find it.

Perhaps the fierce winds blew them there or perhaps Some-one was showing them the way. At any rate, they did find shelter on one of the worst winter days I have ever seen. They spent the rest of the winter near it, feeding on the grain spread out for them, as well as wild grapes and the seeds of wild plants such as red-root, lambs-quarter and chicory. Winter did not seem so difficult now, even to me, as I thought of the pheasants safe and well fed, no longer troubled by the storms.

The poor and the helpless have fled to you and have been safe in time of trouble. You give them shelter from storms and shade from the burning heat.

Isaiah 25:4

Good Bread

The fragrance of homemade bread is one of the joys of the winter kitchen. Turning out a high, light loaf of bread with a tender crumb and a good brown crust is one of the most rewarding accomplishments of the householder.

From my own experience I can say that it is not always an easy accomplishment. Several years ago, feeling unsatisfied with the bread I was making, I consulted the culinary department of the library in a nearby city. I spent most of my spare time that winter reading books on bread-making and trying out recipes in the books. I picked up a good many hints on making good bread, including methods for making a good sponge (in bread-making this is *not* the article that's used for cleaning purposes).

I would not say that my efforts to improve my skills gained too much sympathy from my friends. One friend told me, "You just sort of learn by doing. It helps if you can find some real bread flour." Another, a bachelor, showed up one day with a loaf of bread just out of the oven. As I shamelessly started eating this delicious bread right on the spot, he said in an offhand manner that he "just used the recipe on the flour sack."

But I went faithfully back to my books and am happy to say that I can now turn out some fine yeast breads: a French-Canadian cornmeal bread that goes especially well with soups, an oatmeal-honey bread, an enchanting taos pumpkin bread, and a feathery light white potato bread. Then, too, I learned to make raised biscuits (often called "riz biscuits" in the days of yesteryear). They are so simple and so good spread with butter and honey that I often make them for supper, and the recipe is as follows:

Raised Biscuits

1 pkg. dry yeast
1 cup warm buttermilk
½ teaspoon baking soda
2½ cups flour
1 teaspoon salt
2 tablespoons sugar
½ cup shortening

Mix yeast and buttermilk. Add soda. Cut shortening into dry ingredients. Slowly mix liquid mixture into dry mixture. Roll and cut out biscuits. Let stand long enough to rise. Bake about 12 minutes in 425 degree oven.

Bread, of whatever kind, is one of the essentials of life. Jesus used it to teach us how to pray and he used it to tell us something about himself. By holding a fragment of ordinary bread in our hands we find that Jesus is not unknown and unapproachable. He is close at hand to be with us in our struggles, our inadequacies, our accomplishments and our failures.

He sat down to eat with them, took the bread, and said the blessing; then he broke the bread and gave it to them. Then their eyes were opened and they recognized him, but he disappeared from their sight.

Luke 24:30-31

Vines

When God is the gardener he arranges his gardens with ingenuity and imagination. The wild grapevines have been breathtaking this year, climbing over bushes and shrubs and high up into trees along the hedgerows. In the autumn their pale yellow leaves drifted down to the ground like a benediction. Purple grapes, some fierce and wild in flavor, others almost as mild as cultivated grapes, festoon the vines. Some are close to the ground and easy to pick and others are high up in the trees out of reach of human hands but convenient for the birds.

Opossums and skunks, raccoons and the foxes pick off the ones near the ground, deer browse on the head-high ones. Squirrels and robins, mourning doves and partridge feed on the higher ones. Now in the frozen days of winter the grapes are shriveled and dried out, something like raisins, and full of nourishment. Almost every day as I pass by a hedgerow on my way to the spring, a partridge explodes with heart-stopping alarm out of a canopy of grapevines where it has been resting and feeding.

At a time when I was working in the city at a children's home, I picked a sack full of some especially mild grapes growing in a hedgerow on the farm. Since one of my duties was taking the smaller girls on nature walks, I thought they might enjoy eating the grapes on our next nature outing. (I felt sorry for city children who had no access to these splendid country joys.) Our next outing took place in an area devoted to a park and a zoo. The children helped themselves to the wild grapes and all went well until we came to an outdoor deer enclosure. The little girls all decided that the deer would love the grapes, too. So they held succulent bunches through the bars and the deer thrust their soft muzzles into their hands and fed happily until the grapes were all gone. They had probably never had such a delicacy before in their carefully regulated lives.

I was most uneasy, however, for I had noticed a stern warning sign against feeding the deer, with threats of fines, jail and so on if the notice was not heeded. But the girls were as busy as a covey of little quail and it was impossible to stop their activity. Fortunately no one noticed us and the bountiful grape harvest was enjoyed in some unexpected places that day.

Jesus is the true vine and his father is the gardener. We abide in him and he in us and we cannot bear fruit if we separate ourselves from our Savior.

I am the real vine and my Father is the gardener. . .A branch cannot bear fruit by itself, it can do so only if it remains in the vine.

John 15:1

Catalogs

January is the month when the homesteader spreads the new garden catalogs out on the kitchen table and makes out the orders for the coming growing season. The seed merchants cannily send their catalogs through the mails when the harsh winds are stirring up swirling snow devils in the old road and the numbing cold seems ready to last forever. We need the pictures of shining rows of ruby red beets, jade green cabbages, wonderfully tender green beans. No matter that last year the muskmelon didn't germinate very well, a rabbit leveled our delightful butter crunch lettuce, and the dog lay down for a nap on the squash vines. This year things will be different. And one has discovered a company that carries the rare Gilfeather turnip seed, a Vermont specialty, that produces turnips especially tender and delicately flavored, a joy to look forward to.

Some of the seed will fall on stony soil. Some will fall among thorn bushes (huge burdock and thistle plants that pull up so hard). They lean over into the vegetables and steal sunlight, nutrients and rain water. But some will fall on good soil and with steady hoeing, weeding and watering, there should be a fine crop of butter-and-sugar sweet corn and delicious Lincoln peas and bright golden carrots. Maybe this would even be a good year to build a cold frame so that the growing season can be extended a bit, for the climate here can sometimes be unkind to tender plants.

Some of it fell on rocky ground where there was little soil. The seeds soon sprouted, because the soil wasn't deep. Then when the sun came up, it burned the young plants and because the roots had not grown deep enough, the plants soon dried up.

Mark 4:5-6

Cracking Nuts

Sometimes on the cold stormy January evenings I crack some hickory nuts on an old anvil that I keep handy in the living room for this purpose. Then I settle down with a nut-pick and an old graniteware plate of the cracked nuts and pry out the nut meats that are so delicious in cakes and cookies and maple sugar fudge. A friend brought a grocery box full of nuts to me in December. She had picked them up near her cottage on the shore of the St. Lawrence River.

At Christmas time we sometimes have quite a problem with gifts. We try to find presents that our loved ones will like but often our judgment is faulty and a bit later on the stores do a brisk business in exchanging gifts. Also we usually try to spend about the same amount on the presents we give as we think will be spent on those we receive. But the gift of the hickory nuts was a gift from the heart, freely given, that I could never really repay. So it is with God's gift to us of his Son, with no conditions of repayment. A response of love and hope is aroused in each one of us when we know at last that we are loved that much.

Let us praise God for his glorious grace, for the free gift he gave us in his dear Son.

Ephesians 1:6

Soul Food

Snoopy, the beloved comic strip beagle, often begins the perpetual book that he is working on with the phrase, "It was a dark and stormy night." I'm afraid mine are apt to begin with the words, "It was a cold and stormy winter's day." Actually, we do have mild, sunny winter days and my great-grandmother always said that she could "smell spring" when the days began to lengthen in January. Well, anyway it *was* cold and stormy the other day when I waded through the heavy snow out to the bird-feeding station. I was carrying a supply of provender for what the bird seed companies always refer to as "our feathered friends." A cheerful little chickadee fluttered down from a nearby cedar tree and perched on my fingers, his wings brushing my hand so lightly that they might well have been angel wings. My handful of cracked corn, wheat, milo and millet was briskly inspected, at first with an air of complacent confidence, which rapidly disintegrated into alarm. The small bird hopped up to my wrist, which it clutched with its frail but sharp claws, peering with concern into my face. Chickadee, I decided, making a lucky guess, wanted to see if this heretofore dependable person realized that his beloved sunflower seeds were missing. So I hastily dug down into the feed pail and remedied this situation.

It was quite easy to provide a miscellaneous collection of food for the hungry little bird but harder to supply the innermost needs and longings of my small winged friend's spirit—in this particular case, sunflower seeds.

. . . I tell you that even if he will not get up and give you the bread because you are his friend, yet he will get up and give you everything you need because you are not ashamed to keep on asking.

Luke 11:8

Friends

The January sky can be awesome and forbidding when storm clouds are piling up in the west. On clear, cold days it is a bright, deep blue and whether it is the lowness of the sun or the purity of the air, the shadows that the sun casts on the snow in January are a lovely, unique shade of blue-gray.

On a mild January day when the maple branches are a delicate tracery of soft charcoal against the sky I notice that a porcupine has climbed up into a maple tree and seems to be slumbering there. I always had thought that my little road was out of the way without much travel, but all through the day there are rappings on my door and people (snowmobilers, the mailman, the oil delivery man, the feed store salesman and so on) ask me excitedly if I know that there is a porcupine in my maple tree. They seem to think I should do something about it. But I do not really have any plans to do anything about my guest, who no doubt wandered there from the nearby woods.

When the winter dusk moves in quickly as it does in January I see the porcupine still up in the tree, a small huddled dark form under the tent that God spread out for his entire creation.

He stretched out the sky like a curtain, like a tent in which to live.
Isaiah 40:22

The Pileated Woodpecker

Sometimes we get so concerned with the trials and diffi-culties of life that we fail to appreciate God's providence in our lives and the beauties of his creation. On a January afternoon I am busy moving snow. The garage, the mailbox and a pathway to the road all need shoveling out. After working for awhile my arms are tired, my fingers have chil-blains and a mass of snow falls from a tree limb down on to my head, working with chilly fingers down inside my coat collar.

I remember the neat, hand-shoveled paths my grandfather always kept around his farmstead on the edge of a little hamlet in the snowy Champion Hills. He never just climbed over tramped-down snow drifts as I sometimes do. It was always a joy to walk along his well-cleared paths and I still wonder how he managed to maintain them.

Then I hear a loud clattering call made by a pileated woodpecker as he flies through the wintry gloom into the side yard where he hammers away on a maple branch. His crest is a blaze of scarlet, the color of dragon's blood or of embers of coal bursting into flame. I think how fortunate I am. If I had not been out shoveling snow I would not have seen this beautiful bird.

God has many ways of opening our eyes and setting us free from the dark prisons where we sometimes dwell—a glimpse into the mystery of his creation, the helpful words of a friend, or a bit of quiet insight into the meaning of life.

You will open the eyes of the blind and set free those who sit in dark prisons.

Isaiah 42:7

Trails

Now in January the snow is heavy and deep and I can look across from the farm buildings to a ridge of high land and see fox trails. If I look over in the late afternoon the trail breaker himself can often be seen, trotting over the ridgeline and down the southern side along his paths, the sun gleaming on his thick red coat and tail tipped with white. He makes detours, pouncing into brush piles and tussocks, nosing about under the fragrant pine trees that grow there, finally disappearing into the purple shadows along a small creek. There is something about higher ground that the fox loves. He likes to travel along the hills and ridges.

The messenger I see on this winter's day tells me something about the beauty and the wonder of God's creation. In second Isaiah, a messenger is seen coming across the mountains, bringing good news of the peace of God, a message especially timely now when we long for God's peace in a world overburdened with nuclear arms. God's beautiful creation could be destroyed if we do not search out the ways of peace with God's help.

How wonderful it is to see a messenger coming across the mountains, bringing good news, the news of peace!

Isaiah 52:7

Night Visitor

One frigid January evening I came across an opossum friend in the shed. His eyes glowed a lovely dull-orange in the beam of the flashlight, and he looked rather spooky with his white face and quiet ways. Indeed the Indians used to call him the white beast. He's really very beautiful, with his long, fluffy silky-grey coat.

He is a strange little animal, though, and I often see his curious, small, starfish-like tracks meandering around the yard. Right now he is enjoying a peanut-butter sandwich and some apple slices that were set out for him earlier in the evening.

The opossum dates back in fossil records to the Upper Cretaceous Time, about 120 million years ago, a time when the great dinosaurs were fading away and most primitive marsupials were just developing. So he has been around for awhile, an especially tenacious and adaptable little animal, but, never before has he been in a world where fifty-thousand nuclear warheads are pointed at each other. We can only believe that the hairs on his head (coat) are all numbered, and ours are too, by One who loves us all.

Aren't five sparrows sold for two pennies? Yet not one sparrow is forgotten by God...Even the hairs of your head have all been counted. So do not be afraid.

Luke 12:6

Cows and Beets

Recently I was reading in a diary for the year 1886, kept by a ten-year-old boy who lived at that time in my old farmhouse. In his entry for January 9 he wrote, "Very cold. Everything is freezing up, I cut the beets for the cow, a bushel, and fed them to her." I became quite alarmed at the idea of one cow getting herself around a whole bushel of beets and skipped ahead to see if there was any further mention of the cow, especially in regard to her health. Everything must have been all right, for on January 17 he wrote, "I cut the beets for the old cow today and fed them to her." I should have had more faith in the boy, growing up on the farm and taught by his father how to care for the different kinds of livestock that they kept.

Since then I have looked into the usage of beets as a cattle as well as sheep food. In a textbook on feeding by Prof. Morrison of Cornell I found that the chief nutrients in roots (beets, mangels, sugar beets, carrots, parsnips or potatoes) are carbohydrates and that they also are high in niacin. A pound of dry matter in roots usually equals a pound of dry matter in grain. Sometimes they have been fed as a relish to animals being fitted for show, and also to cows on official test.

I also found that the dry matter in roots is of a high quality, being low in fiber, highly digestible and high in net energy per pound. They have been used very extensively as a livestock food in Great Britain and northern European countries where the summers are cool and corn does not do well. While they are not fed very much in this country today, my local Agway man says that the growing number of sheep people in the area often buy beet pulp to feed them when they are planning to exhibit their sheep, as it makes them look especially nice and thrifty.

"Now that you have known me," he said to them, "you will know my Father also, and from now on you do know him and you have seen him."

John 14:7

January Thaw

The 40th Psalm is a lovely song of praise to God and thanksgiving for his saving strength in time of danger. Instead of burnt offerings, the psalmist says that God wants us to listen to him and keep his teachings in our hearts.

What do I hear when I listen to him? On this winter's morning there is mildness in the air and I hear the eaves dripping. Several big icicles by the back door have loosened their grip enough so that they fall down into the snow with soft thuds. I break them into small pieces with a wooden mallet and add them to the barrel where I store the melted snow water that I use for household chores. Icicles make nice, clean, soft water.

In the hen house the hens croon and cluck with a new joyful confidence. They gently peck my fingers when I reach under them in the straw-filled nests to collect the eggs. They are enjoying the respite from the cold which for days has been so severe it was as if all life was stretched taut almost to its breaking point. The two stray cats sit on a sunlit windowsill in the little shed and purr with pleasure, letting the warmth flood deep into their bones.

What do I hear when I listen for him? I hear the sounds of his creation affirming that his world is good. There may be difficulties and hardships but if we trust in him the bleak times will not last forever. There will be a time to sing a new song In our lIves.

Instead you have given me ears to hear you, and so I answered, "Here I am; your instructions for me are in the book of the Law."

Psalm 40:6-7

All The Way Down

Several years ago I was preparing an article for a small country newspaper on that delightful recreation of sliding downhill. I expected that it would be easy to interview my neighbors and their children and dig up a lot of exciting sliding tales. I was wrong, for I found that television watching or snowmobile riding in this area, at least, has mostly replaced my favorite winter sport. This was quite a disappointment.

Eventually I stopped at the home of an elderly friend, a reliable guru on rural matters, and asked him what he knew about going downhill fast. He said he didn't know much because he had never been interested in sliding downhill himself. However, he went on to tell me about a time when he was only twelve, living on the farm where he still lives today. A sleet storm had sheathed all the world in ice overnight. His parents were young and full of fun and could not look upon this spectacle without doing something about it. They had no real sled so they thought of the little pung. This was a homely, normally slow-going little sleigh used for jobs around the farm. There were broad runners with a wooden box set on the runners, and since it was intended to be horse drawn, there was no means of steering it. Around the farm it was used to clean the barn, to break trail for the cattle or sheep to the creek for water, and even to go to the village for supplies when deep fingers of snow drifted across the roads. His folks dragged the pung to the top of the long range of hills which rise above the farmstead toward the east.

They seated themselves upon the pung, pushed off, and came down the hills in one careless, glorious ride that went on almost forever and ended down in the valley near the banks of Sandy Creek. Ordinary obstacles such as fences, rocks, streams, roads and hedge rows slipped by or were run over by the head-strong little pung as if they were of no consequence. It had taken his parents an hour to pull the pung back home where they soberly put it away and never used it again, at least as a recreational vehicle.

There is a verse in the book of Ezekiel that says *I felt the powerful presence of the Lord and heard Him say to me, "Get up and go out into the valley. I will talk to you there."* It occurred to me that there are all sorts of ways to get out into the valley.

At the Water's Edge

Besides the 1886 diary of the young boy who once lived in the farm house, I also have in my possession a diary kept in 1884 by his father. His entry for February 19th noted, "It has snowed quite hard all day. We have not had a worse day this winter. Mr. Cagwin has my cutter and buffalo (robe) and Mr. Patrick has the light bobs (a type of sleigh) and the kettle (to help break open roads) is at Pa's. Poped corn tonight." (The young father often mentioned through the wintertime that he popped corn, and always spelled it with just the one "p".)

He seemed quite undisturbed by the wide dispersal of his winter traveling equipment so necessary for any movement at all over the snow-drifted roads which were unattended, of course, by the plows that keep our present day roads open most of the time.

Some of us spend considerable time along the shoreline, worrying about the frequency and size of the waves that roll in, after we cast our bread upon the waters; but not this generous-hearted young farmer.

Cast thy bread upon the waters: for thou shalt find it after many days.

Ecclesiastes 11:1

Peanut Butter

Recently I happened to be shopping in a small family-run grocery store. Even though small, it had a really nice selection of fresh fruits and vegetables, dairy products, crackers, cheeses and so on. A smartly dressed young woman turned to a little boy about four years old, who was holding her hand, and told him that they would have to go home for lunch as it was almost 12 o'clock. Then, thoughtfully regarding the grocery shelves, she asked him what he wanted her

to buy for their lunch. The little boy happily shouted, "PEA-
NUT BUTTER!"

This answer would certainly have pleased George Washington Carver, the great scientist who after the Civil War im-
mensely improved the faltering economy of the South by
developing in his laboratory all kinds of uses for the nutritious
peanut, including peanut butter. But it did not please the
young mother. "I certainly will not get you any more peanut
butter," she declared. "All you ever want is peanut butter."
And the exasperated mother dragged the youngster, now
screeching and sobbing, out of the store and that is the last
that I saw of them.

So it often is, even when we are much older than the little
boy, that our best hopes and dreams meet with disappointment. We may lose our loved ones, homes, jobs, beloved
pets, and even our health. There may seem to be nothing
left in the world that makes life worth the bother. But there
is always ONE to whom we can take these losses and failures,
blighted hopes and mislaid dreams, our Savior Jesus Christ.
He will heal our sorrows and help us to find a new dream,
firmly grounded in the reality of his loving presence in our
lives.

Come unto me all ye who labor and are heavy laden.
Matthew 1:28

Treasure

In a letter that Paul wrote to God's people in Ephesus, he
reminded them that God's power is at work in all those who
believe. Sometimes we wonder about this power and what it
is like, for we do not always feel very powerful. However, the
power of God is all around us. We cannot fail to know about
it if we study his word with a thoughtful spirit.

Down by the pond I find a cocoon of the Cecropia moth.
It is large and fluffy, made with pale golden silk firmly

anchored with more silken strands to a small thornapple sapling, on the side away from the prevailing winds. There must be a great creative power silently at work in the cocoon for the caterpillar that spun this lovely little sepulchre will emerge in early summer, no longer a caterpillar but rearranged into a beautiful moth that will float like a dream on the gentle winds of the velvety dark, warm nights.

Perhaps we need to know how to use this power from God. If so, we might remember the story Jesus told about a man who found treasure buried in a field and gave up everything to buy the field so that the treasure would be his. God put into the man's heart the willingness to give up all of his old possessions to buy the field.

He does the same with us today. His power enables us to put away the old unhappy memories of our failures, lost dreams, and blemished actions and to go forward with love, happiness and courage, for we have found a new life in Christ.

And how very great is his power at work in us who believe.'
Ephesians 1:19

On the Road

There has been a snowfall in the night leaving several inches of fluffy new snow on the ground. As I drive down my small road I notice that I am fast approaching a bird standing in the middle of the road pecking up bits of grit. I know that there is someone whose eye is on the sparrow and I do not want him to think that I would run over a lovely pine grosbeak, one of his own. As I wait, the grosbeak flies up into a highbush cranberry by the roadside to feed on the ruby-red fruits that still cling to the bush. The sun shines on the glowing raspberry red of the bird's breast as he fluffs out his feathers in the cold and the snow falls from the twigs in little sparkling showers of diamonds. What fine beautiful sights one can see just driving down an old road!

On another road long ago Paul was seized with wonder and awe and perhaps some guilt when our Savior appeared to him and changed his life forever. From a life dedicated to the fierce unraveling of the Christian faith, Paul became the apostle to the gentiles. He would one day write, "I may be able to speak the languages of men and even of angels, but if I have no love, my speech is no more than a noisy gong or a clanging bell. I may have the gift of inspired preaching; I may have all knowledge and understand all secrets; I may have all the faith needed to move mountains. . .but if I have no love, I am nothing."

May we, too, meet our Savior in this new year and come to love him so well that we could not imagine life without him.

It was on the road at midday, your majesty, that I saw a light much brighter than the sun coming from the sky and shining around me. . .and I heard a voice say to me in Hebrew, "Saul, Saul! Why are you persecuting me?"

Acts 26:13-14

By Lantern Light

Electricity did not come to our farm until I was in my teens and in those earlier years my father always carried a lantern to the barn for the evening chores and milking. He hung it on a stout nail high up on a beam where it could not be tipped over and its mellow, steady glow lighted up the stable to what seemed to me then a great sufficiency of light. We had plenty of light to milk by hand the gentle, dark-eyed Jersey cows, to shake out fresh straw beneath their feet, fork out fragrant hay into the manger in front of them, and feed the calves.

Finally, after everything was done, my father lifted the lantern down off the nail and opened the barn door to the cold, starry night and we went back to the house for our supper. In those days the stable by the glow of the lantern seemed to me to be a safe, secure place where nothing could possibly harm me, and my father could solve any problems that might appear. Now I know that my father was really subject to many problems and had little real security in case anything went wrong or the crops failed. But I will always remember the steady, life-giving light of the lantern as it shone in our stable and brought a sense of peace and safety no matter how badly wild blizzards or sleety rains might shake the barn.

Does anyone ever bring in a lamp and put it under a bowl or under the bed? Doesn't he put it on the lampstand?

Mark 4:21

Songs

The songs of wintertime are different than the songs of springtime and summer, but they are beautiful, too. They speak of the wild places, of drifting snows and fierce winds, of days and nights when we stay close to the comfort of our beleagured homes.

About 3 o'clock this morning two Great Horned Owls were perched somewhere in the trees around the house calling with their beautiful, muffled, "whoos," a wild song that often seems to foretell the falling of more snow. My dog, hearing them in her dreams no doubt, awoke and became so agitated I feared she might go out through a window, so I hastily arose and let her out the door. She barked in the moonlight-flooded yard until the owls must have drifted off on mighty wings to more peaceful surroundings, for eventually the night was silent again.

With whatever song we have in our hearts we praise our Creator for his providence and love through the days and nights of his year as we move from the green, flowering days

of summer through the mellow, misty days of autumn, the cold snowy days of winter when the stars sparkle with edges like cut glass, and on to the lovely promising days of springtime.

Give praise to the Lord; he has heard my cry for help. The Lord protects and defends me; I trust in him. He gives me help and makes me glad; I praise him with joyful songs.

Psalm 28:6-7

The Color Red

During the ministry of Jesus, the Pharisees and others watched closely to see if he would break the Law by healing on the sabbath. They did not seem to doubt that Jesus had the power to heal, but their entire attention was given to the matter of trapping him in an infraction of the law. And so one sabbath day when Jesus entered the synagogue he found a man with a paralyzed hand. Jesus took him to the front of the room where everyone could see what was happening and healed him.

It would probably have been easier for Jesus to tell this man to wait for another day. But Jesus needed to make his followers understand that a simple loving spirit was more important than a complicated, arid set of rules in which both God and man had largely been forgotten. Then, too, Jesus meets us where he finds us, in trouble, fallen by the wayside. We do not have to wait for a more convenient time to know his saving, healing power.

The healing touch of God can come at any time. I feel the touch of God on a cold winter's day when I see a cardinal up in the larch tree calling a clearly whistled "whe-at" and feeding on seeds he is picking out of the little cones. His scarlet feathers glow in the sunshine, a beautiful contrast to the scalloped drifts of pure white snow beneath the tree.

Thank you, God, especially in the wintertime, for the color red. The blazing red of a cardinal, the weatherbeaten red of the old barn, the dusky red of the little storage chest in the kitchen that was made by my great-grandfather, the warm red flames in my little wood stove.

Then Jesus went back to the synagogue where there was a man who had a paralyzed hand...Then he said to the man, "Stretch out your hand." He stretched it out and it became well again.

Mark 3:1-5

Windows

This is the time of year when we can expect the snow and the cold and the piercing winds. In the little farmhouse in the beautiful Champion Hills where I spent my early childhood, the windows with their small panes of streaked, bubbly glass were often covered with lovely frost flowers and ferns in the wintertime. One hardly ever sees frost flowers anymore, as our windows are protected so well both inside and out with storm windows, insulating shades and plastic. But in those days we just had simple roller shades that pulled down to the windowsill.

With a warm wood fire inside and the intense cold directly outside the glass, conditions especially at night time were right for the formation for thick frost crystals. A hundred degrees or so might separate the world beyond the window-pane from the comforting warmth by the fireside. It was very absorbing for us children to watch the flowers and plants of spring and summertime appear in fanciful designs on the windows. Sometimes we blew on the windows or traced the designs with our fingertips, watching them melt under our touch and then reappear when we removed our hands. Was this not a sign from God saying, "Behold I am here. I will make your window especially beautiful so that you will remember me"?

I may not see frost flowers on my windows this winter but

some things never change through the years, such as God's love and providence for all of his creation and the star that leads us to Bethlehem.

He spreads snow like a blanket and scatters frost like dust. He sends hail like gravel; no one can endure the cold he sends.
Psalm 147:16-17

Apple Trees

After raging all morning, the snowstorm that started yesterday has finally spent itself now at 2 p.m. The radio weatherman says that three feet of lake-effect snow have fallen since the storm began. Some of my windows are encased in sheets of snow that gently bulge outward. No doubt the windows are warmer than when the panes of glass were exposed to the cold air and winds.

How good it is that the old apple trees on the pasture hillside have reappeared like old friends after troubled times. How like a miracle it is that these old trees, the Wolf Rivers and the Russets, the Greening, the Dutchess and Transparents, and other varieties of long ago, seem unblemished by the storm which must have hit them full force. I can almost see them crowned in their May-time glory of pink and white as they stand there sturdy against the violet blue horizon of winter.

The Lord is like this, faithful and steady, to be counted upon for help and guidance when we are in doubt or trouble. The psalmist says that the Lord will guard us always. How wonderful to know that we are uplifted by a strength beyond our own.

The protector of Israel never dozes or sleeps. The Lord will guard you; he is by your side to protect you.
Psalm 121:4-5

Winter Nights

Sometimes on bitter cold winter nights when about the only sounds are made by the timbers in the house snapping now and then, and nails popping explosively in the cold, I leave a small lamp burning through the night. This little circle of brightness seems to give me the courage and hope to get safely through another night in my isolated rural home. Sometimes I even get up for awhile, put another chunk of wood on the fire, knit or read and maybe brew a cup of coffee in the middle of the night. I let the cat out for a few minutes and attend to my household chores as if it were day. Sometimes I even go out and fill the poultry feeders in readiness for a new day. When the snowplow comes up, its yellow warning lights flashing on the kitchen ceiling at about 5 o'clock in the morning and the beautiful morning star of Venus glows in the east, I blow out the lamp and with new hope and confidence go back to bed for several hours of sleep.

The message of God is like the lamp shining through the dark hours of the night. How can the shadows and darkness and difficulties of life defeat us when we have this bright beam of light to guide us on our way?

Your word is a lamp to guide me and a light for my path.
                                                            Psalm 119:105

Crows in Heaven?

On a mild, sunny day in early March the crows are flying busily about, inspecting the boundaries of their far-flung properties. Enthusiastic, abundantly visible, and highly voluble again after a long cold winter when there was only a distant caw now and then from way back in the woods. Old timers thought that this noisy reappearance of the crows was a sign that the maple sugar season was at hand—a propitious time to tap the trees, hang the buckets, and maybe get up a little more firewood for the boiling. I suspect they were right, for certainly the air has the feel of golden sap-flow in it now.

As I watch the crows, I think of my father who remarked many times that he thought heaven would be a dull place indeed if there were no crows in residence. (This from a farmer who for many years raised popcorn as a cash crop to "help out" the milk checks and had to contrive all sorts of ingenious methods to outwit the crows, who also truly cherished popcorn.) I think he feared just a little that heaven might be sort of a boring place. After all, we do hear a lot about choirs of angels constantly singing, great white thrones and golden streets. In our heart of hearts some of us have to admit that this could all get just a little tiresome.

I have thought considerably about this and have come to the conclusion that God who made the hummingbird, the golden-winged honeybees, the beautiful scarlet-orange of the climbing bittersweet, and the mischievous coal-black crow, could not possibly be responsible for putting together a dull, monotonous heaven.

There are many rooms in my Father's house, and I am going to prepare a place for you. I would not tell you this if it were not so.

John 14:2

Testing the Maple Sap

Maple syrup-making has a long and honorable history in my family. I still have in my possession the old wooden sap buckets and quaint iron spiles that once belonged to my great-grandfather. My father, in a fervor of patriotic anxiety to be off to the First World War, was finally prevailed upon by his parents to wait until the sugaring season was over. And he in turn, as a young farmer, always made syrup in the springtime.

He had a hired man, or to put it more correctly, a man who could sometimes be hired, to help him out in the sugaring season. This rather eccentric and cranky little man was a friend and neighbor who lived on a small farm of his own, and was much better off financially than my father. Being of a frugal nature anyway, and having quite a sizeable inheritance from adoptive parents, he lived as he called it, "mostly out of the bank." Indeed, on several occasions my father in his precarious early years of farming borrowed money from our friend and sometime hired hand, Gene.

Gene had no real need to work out, but he liked my father, and also my mother's good home cooking, and sometimes could be prevailed upon to help out during the sugaring, haying, grain-threshing and wood-cutting seasons. He had another farmer whom he sometimes helped out especially at sugaring time. My father was always in a state of uncertainty as to whether he or Hank Loomis was going to benefit in any given year from Gene's assistance. Therefore, my father had rather a competitive feeling about the respective merits of the two sugar operations. In the years that Gene did help my father during the exigencies of making syrup, my father would always inquire hopefully if his syrup was as good as Hank Loomis's. "Gosh, no!" Gene always exclaimed, while refreshing himself with brimming dippers of the boiling sap (cooled down a little by holding it in the brisk cold spring air for a bit before drinking).

In all of the years of syrup making, until we moved to our lakeside farm that was devoid of sugar maples, my father's optimistic idea that perhaps *this* year he had surpassed Hank Loomis, was always firmly squelched. But, deep down in his heart, he knew that it was really fine syrup, and he was not truly downcast. It was more like a game that he thought sometime he might win. And nobody can really be bothered by small setbacks when there is a good run of sap, the fires in the evaporator are roaring, and wild geese are skeining northward overhead. There are some enterprises where it is just natural that,

You will be as happy as those who walk to the music of flutes
on their way to the temple of the Lord, the defender of Israel.
Isaiah 30:27

Spring Peepers

It was late March and I mentioned to a friend that I had just heard the very first spring peepers calling tentatively, almost questioningly, from a nearby pond. "Spring peeper! What's that?" she wanted to know. I could hardly believe that someone who had always lived in the country did not know what a spring peeper was. With considerable difficulty I began to explain, "Well, it is a little tree frog..." "Oh Ilene, you know all these outdoor things. You're going to have to teach me," she interrupted enthusiastically. And then she rushed on to some other subject before I could proceed any further with my discourse on the spring peeper.

Perhaps this was just as well. How to describe this tiny frog, not just any big green frog, but a very miniscule one, only about as big as the end of my thumb. And the bit of gold around its eyes and the dark cross on the back which accounts for its name, Hyla Crucifer, which, translated into English is Cross-Bearer. Then there is the magic when you first hear them calling in the springtime. There is probably still some ice in the ponds and marshes but the air has just a token hint of mildness and the pussy-willows are a soft, silky gray.

When you hear them calling you can almost see the earth millions of years ago, with the peepers adding their noise to the primeval chaos. Or perhaps you remember more recent times—the midsummer day when you found one sitting inside a moist decayed hollow stump looking very small and placid; or the golden hued autumn day when one was found clinging to a blackberry bramble. For these little tree frogs return to land when springtime fades into summer, and are mostly silent then except sometimes for a little minor resurgence of calling after a dry spell has been broken by rain, or in the autumn. It is only by accident that one sees them after they leave the pond, or even in the pond for that matter. A human footstep can silence an entire pond of spring peepers and their chiming, bell-like notes.

I know it would have been difficult to make all of this something real and beautiful to my friend. And I wonder if God ever finds it difficult to tell our human hearts about his love, his Son, his kingdom. Perhaps he does it in stages—a courteous kindness from the man who repairs my car, a smile from the girl who handles my account so carefully in the bank, a bed of King Alfred daffodils nodding in the restless spring air. Perhaps a scrubby little plant at the rummage sale, that needs tender care: a lonely child who needs someone to listen to him and bolster his self-esteem with cookies and milk. Even the little stray dog whose next stop will be the pound unless we take it into our hearts.

Thou sendest forth thy spirit . . . Thou renewest the face of the earth.

Psalm 104:30

Where the Palaces Are

The maple sugar season is here again and at the garden there is a good deal of commotion as I attempt to keep ahead of the steady flow of sap. Sugaring is a very socially acceptable pastime and there are usually some friends and neighbors sitting on the sturdy pieces of stump wood that I have arranged near the fireplace just for this purpose. Or sometimes they perch on the makeshift plank table where I keep odds and ends of syrup equipment and various supplies.

They enjoy the fragrant steamy aroma rising from the syrup pan, and are dipped up frequent samples of the developing product. They often dreamily remark that they used to get some real light syrup up around Croghan, or the other side of Harrisville. (These are areas with a reputation for almost mystically light syrup, possibly due to the composition of the soil.) The same is often said of Theresa and there the almost luminous pale color is thought to be due to the maples growing "so close to the rock".

I have made some improvements to the simple lot of the backyard sugar maker, but a recent visitor, after watching the scene for awhile, observed patiently, "You should see the sugar shanties over in Lewis County. They're palaces."

From start to finish the sugaring season is an exciting time. Who is better positioned than the sugar maker to hear the first wild geese passing overhead, to hear the special trembling "ice is out" roar from the nearby creek, to notice a Mourning Cloak butterfly, awake at last and flying strongly in the warm sunshine, and now to hear news of palaces over in the next county?

The queen of Sheba heard Solomon's wisdom and saw the palace he had built . . . It left her breathless and amazed.
2 Chronicles 9:3-4

Loneliness

One of the major problems of society today is loneliness. Anyone who has ever conducted a maple sugaring operation, boiling down maple sap and then "sugaring off" has probably noticed that this activity brings company to the woodlot, putting an end to loneliness.

A young farmer who once lived in my cherished old farmhouse noted in his diary for March 28, 1884, that "Mrs. Cagwin and her children came over to the sugar shanty and got some warm sugar to eat." And another day "Mrs. Brown, Lucinda, Willie, Christy, and Herb Smith all came here to have warm sugar." The young farmer seemed glad to have visitors to his sugar bush and did not seem to mind at all that they hadn't been there to empty the heavy sap buckets, cut firewood, tend the fire in the sap house, and perhaps clean up a pan of burnt sugar (a hazard of sugar making). It is hard to be stingy when the sap is running, the sugar house is clouded with a pleasant steamy fragrance, and spring is sneaking in the back door.

Gold and silver are tested by fire, and a person's heart is tested by the Lord.

Proverbs 17:3

Bees in the Cellar

On an early day in April the sunshine is hot by mid-afternoon. The thermometer stands at 65 degrees on the shaded east side of the cabin. Down around the pond the silvery gray pussywillow buds are in bloom full of tiny, golden-yellow flowers. The lengthening days, the warm sunshine and the gentle spring winds have all worked their magic and now the willow bushes are humming with honey bees. In this northern area, the pussywillows are about the earliest source of nectar as well as the pollen needed to feed the early brood in the hive. Somehow the bees, clustered around the honeycomb in the hive, were told the good news that the flowers were opening.

In years past, on northern farms, bees were often overwintered down in the cellars. In those days before central heating, the cellars were cool and dark, a good place for the bees to pass the tedious winter days.

The young farmer who lived in the farmhouse in 1884 made an entry for November 26 as follows: "I went over home to help carry the bees down cellar but they were carried down yesterday." One hopes that the owner of the cellared bees kept track of the willow swales, and brought the bees outdoors when the time was right for their first spring flights. It would have been hard for the little sisters of the hive to be cooped up when they knew it was that lovely season—spring.

Son, eat honey, it is good. And just as honey from the comb is sweet on your tongue, you may be sure that wisdom is good for the soul. Get wisdom, and you have a bright future.

Proverbs 24:13-14

Falling Stones

Part of my childhood farm was what we called "the stone house place." It had once been a small separate farm but it had been bought and added to the larger one. The stone farmhouse fell into disuse. It was exquisite, with hand-cut, native limestone walls laid up with loving care, two stone fireplaces, and a broad front doorstep of stone.

The homestead was sheltered by gentle hills and groves and valleys from the harshest winds, and watered by springs and a pleasant creek. In early spring before winter had been routed in most of the countryside, the grass there became green and fresh while other grasses at other farms still lay flattened and dingy with the burden of winter's debris. The house, however, gradually fell apart. Even occasional repairs could not stop its steady deterioration by the weather, aided by vandals. When I last saw it there were only remnants of the walls left, the beautiful stones strewn about the green, grassy knoll. Like the temple at Jerusalem, it was gone.

But Jesus did not merely prophesy the destruction of the temple of Jerusalem. He leaves us always with new hope and new faith and he promised us, "Lo, I will be with you always, even unto the ends of the earth."

All this you see—the time will come when not a single stone here will be left in the place; every one will be thrown down.

Luke 21:6

Vultures

For a few days it has been warm and sunny—April on its best behavior. Occasionally I had heard a bird-call from the skies—"scree"—that I could not exactly identify. But today I found the answer when I happened to look up into the warm blue sky and saw two vultures flying their April love song, calling this short, joyful cry that I had been hearing. Vultures' flight is always so beautiful. They fly so effortlessly up there in the heavens, tilting from side to side and when you see one vulture, before long others drift into view, always flying in ever-widening circles. The two vultures I watch today are circling each other, sometimes flying so close that they almost collide.

Vultures are newcomers to my part of New York state. When I was a child they were unknown here but they have moved northward along with cardinal, opossum and some other legendary residents of the southland. Since vultures are scavengers, they do not get a very good press, although they are simply a part of the cycle of building up and breaking down that is all the way the earth works.

They are really only performing the same service as are the delicate, tiny roots of a bedstraw plant that I find growing in a moss-lined, hairline crack in a large pink boulder along the creek. Some day these small roots and other similar ones will break up the boulder into tiny particles that will return to the soil. But even so, a deep prejudice against vultures lingers in the human heart.

Once when I worked for a time as a housemother in a home and school for handicapped children in Virginia I pointed out to another housemother some vultures circling high in the sky. Without too much interest she said resignedly, "Someone's going to die." Well, this may be, but as that austere philosopher of Walden Pond pointed out, if a man is alive there is always *danger* that he may die. If we have been alive to the beauty and love and generosity of God we do not need to fear death. For as Jesus said:

Whoever wants to serve me must follow me, so that my servant will be with me where I am. And my Father will honor anyone who serves me.

John 12:26

Listening

It was an April afternoon and I was sowing some early lettuce seed when I noted that the atmosphere seemed uneasily hushed and strangely quiet for rowdy April. Apparently there were some tricky air currents around, for shortly a whirlwind materialized and settled over the old road where it briskly vacuumed up all of the deep layers of old maple leaves packed against the roadside banks there, sending them flying upward with a banging, rattling roar. The surging, twisting pillar of leaves rose above the tallest maples before it began to subside. For the next hour or so the disarranged leaves were still quietly sifting earthward from the branches where they had been caught.

This seemed like a truly biblical spring scene and I almost expected to hear God speaking from the fearsome center of the whirlwind. But instead I only heard the usual voices of spring—the soft, whistled "whe-at" of a cardinal, the contented clucking of the chickens as they picked over some tender, vitamin-rich mustard greens, the complacent whistle of a woodchuck from his burrow beside the garden, and the mewing of seagulls following the plow in a nearby field.

The Israelites left Sukkath and camped at Etham on the edge of the desert. During the day the Lord went in front of them in a pillar of cloud to show them the way, and during the night he went in front of them in a pillar of fire to give them light, so that they could travel night and day.

Exodus 13:20-22

Bee Song

In late April I walk across a field where oats and barley were raised last year. As yet it has not been plowed up again and it is a sheet of gold, for the dandelions are in full bloom. The blossoms are humming with bee song, little thanksgiving hymns of praise for the dandelion crop, as thousands of honeybees are collecting nectar.

This early nectar helps them to recover from the depletion of their honey stores during our long northern winters. I have been told that dandelion honey is faintly bitter, but it probably is consumed mostly by the bees themselves in the early springtime. Anyway, I think that, like the dandelion itself, it must be full of vitamins and minerals and very tonic for the little golden flying ones.

A year or so ago when I wrote some meditations for *Forward Day by Day* I received a surprising number of letters about a meditation concerning honey (sourwood and basswood). One lovely postcard from Arizona simply said, "Did you ever try mesquite honey?" Being from the northeast I had never thought of mesquite as being a source of honey. Since then, however, I have read that mesquite honey is really delicious. Some people wrote to me from the sourwood honey states. One said, "I live where the bees make sourwood honey." Another mailed me a jar of sourwood honey which I greatly enjoyed on my biscuits and toast.

Buckwheat honey, dark and strongly flavored, is probably at the bottom of the list of favorite honeys. Years ago before modern drainage methods were developed, buckwheat was often the only crop that could be planted on low, wet fields. It could stand a damp, rather sour soil and would come to maturity even when planted late. However, a field of buckwheat in "blow" was not always a welcome sight to any nearby beekeepers. Even a small amount of buckwheat nectar could darken a good deal of the season's honey.

However, buckwheat honey was not scorned by everyone; it was my father's favorite. And I have found that buckwheat or some other dark strong honey is really the best for use in baking. The wild, pungent flavor is moderated in baking to just a pleasant, honey flavor. Lighter honey does not seem to add its lovely, delicate flavor to the baked goods as far as I can see. So here is one of my very favorite recipes, using either buckwheat honey or a strong honey of mixed wildflowers:

Honey Scones

2 cups flour
½ teaspoon salt
4 teaspoons baking powder
6 tablespoons margarine
2 eggs
6 tablespoons honey
½ cup raisins

Mix flour, salt and baking powder. Crumble margarine into this mixture with the fingers. Stir in beaten eggs, honey and raisins. Roll out dough to about ½-inch thick. Cut out scones and brush each with milk on top. Bake about 10 minutes at 425 degrees.

The following were in charge of the singing of hymns of Thanksgiving: Jeshua, Binnui, Kadmiel, Sherebiah, Judah and Mattaniah.

Nehemiah 12:8

Winning

This spring I was in a garage having some work done on my car when I noticed a young lady employee talking to several fellow employees. She was saying, "How come, if I won a trip to the Indy 500, they sent me a ticket to Cincinnati, Ohio?"

This certainly seemed like a reasonable question and along the same lines I found myself thinking, *If we've been promised the kingdom how come we find ourselves traveling many miles each month to visit a loved one in a mental hospital, or serving on a committee that is really quite time-consuming and tedious, or trying without much success to push oversize capsules, that the vet gave us, down the throat of a beloved pet that is terribly sick with pneumonia,* or . . .

Well, maybe this *is* all part of the kingdom of God.

The Pharisees asked Him, "When will the Kingdom of God come?" He said, "You cannot tell by observation when the Kingdom of God comes. There will be no saying 'Look, here it it!'; for in fact the Kingdom of God is among you."
                                                            Luke 17:20-21

Country Problems

Since I live alone in the country, problems often arise that seem impossible to solve by myself. My first thought often is "I'll have to get help." My second thought is, "It would take too long to go and find help. I'll have to figure out something myself." Last spring I was in just such a predicament one day. I had ascended the stairway of a small barn near the farmhouse to hunt up some roofing shingles, as the small cabin roof was in need of some repair work. Lira, my border collie, bounded up the stairs with me, as was her custom. It is a good stairway with a sturdy handrail, built by my father when we first moved to the farm. Before that, the occupants must have propped a ladder from the ground floor up to the larger square opening in the second floor and climbed up the ladder if they needed anything stored away upstairs. I was glad I did not have to do this, as heights make me dizzy.

Lira spent some time exploring the second story with its wide-planked floor, and a few remnants of the farming days of yesteryear. Such as a Myers Kwikfill hand sprayer. This had an attractive advertising label pasted on it. Underneath the heading, "Take off your hat to the Myers Pumps, Water Systems, Hay Tools, and Door Hangers", was a picture of a little girl attired in an old-fashioned turkey-red dress and a flowered sunbonnet. She was pumping water with some sort of an unusual pump that sent a jet of water over to the other side of the advertising label where it was knocking off the cap of a little boy who was trying to carry a pail of water. Apparently, the Myers Company had quite a line of useful farm equipment.

After locating the shingles, I made my way gingerly downstairs again and, thinking that Lira had already gone down the stairs and outside, I shut the door and went about my chores. Before long a strange lonesome feeling settled upon me and I realized that Lira, beloved shadow of all my days, was missing. Of course I remembered that I had actually seen her last in the small barn so I returned there, and opened the door. I could hear her pacing uneasily around overhead. I called, fully expecting her to come rushing down the stairs, but instead she only came to the top and looked down at me in a worried way. I suddenly realized that somehow the years had drifted past and she was now quite an old dog (12). Trotting down those stairs as she had always done in the past no longer seemed to her an easy, fun thing to do.

At first I was really alarmed, sure that I could not manage, as stairs make me dizzy, too. I hoped, however, her love for me would give her the confidence to let me help her. So I ascended to the top, firmly grasped her by the collar, wrapping my arms reassuringly around her neck. Then I started slowly backing down the stairs, pulling her along, keeping my own body between her and all of that empty space below. I told her that it was much easier than it seemed, especially for a very brave dog. Finally, I felt my foot touch the concrete ground floor and we were both safe at last. We sat down on the stone steps and cooled off in the gentle breeze that was sifting through the pale golden haze of maple flowers above, glad for each other's company, glad to be safe again.

Even though my beloved lost one was a dog, I knew just how it would have been in the parable of the lost sheep!

Suppose one of you has a hundred sheep and loses one of them—what does he do? He leaves the other ninety-nine sheep in the pasture and goes looking for the one that got lost until he finds it.

Luke 15:4-5

The Dragons of May

All of the earth is lovely and fragrant now during the Falling Petal Moon of May. And so, amidst all of this new life and beauty it seems so very sad to come across a little salamander, dead in the middle of my old road. It is the yellow-spotted black salamander, supposedly just about extinct now due to acid rain in the northeast. This one, though, was very much alive until it was mortally hurt. I wish there had been another way to find out that these little dragons still live in at least some parts of their range.

I picked it up out of the roadway and laid it beneath a wild Canada plum tree full of fragrant flowers by the roadside, placing a few dried leaves over the strange little body, so still and quiet. The breezes stirred up a few flower petals that fell on the little bier as if in farewell for one of the earth's beloved small creatures. Instead of a fine day exploring the fresh damp goodness of the flowering earth this little one went home again to the loving hands and heart that created him.

Once I would have had hard thoughts about the indifference

of God to let such things happen, or perhaps there is no God and the universe is just one cold, big machine wound up long ago by, who knows? But now I have come to realize that deep in the heart of all life there is pain and sadness, but God broods over it all with a love so deep that we cannot help ourselves from being drawn into that love and sharing it as best we can. Even if it is only to do such a small thing as tucking one of his beloved small creatures away in a tiny sepulchre beneath a wild plum tree that provides a shady spot of restfulness.

> *How precious, O God, is your*
> *constant love!*
> *We find protection under the*
> *shadow of your wings.*
> *We feast on the abundant food*
> *you provide;*
> *You let us drink from the river*
> *of your goodness.*
> *You are the source of all life,*
> *and because of your light we*
> *see the light!*

Psalm 30:7-9

Painted Trilliums

During the beautiful Falling Petal Moon of May I took my annual walk back into a remote area of woods and ravines in search of the painted trillium. This is a handsome and quite uncommon trillium that I found once in these deep woods but which I was never able to locate again. It is an elegant flower with white, wavy-edged petals and a halo of crimson in the center of the flower. I have asked quite a few outdoor-type people if they know of any place where the painted trillium grows. They always say, "Yes," but on running down these leads it has turned out that they were thinking of the red wake-robbins or the white trilliums that turn pinkish with age or, very occasionally, are pinkish even when first opening. So I always go back to my own little private search every springtime. It is possible that the plants have been torn up in logging operations in those woods. Perhaps it is a doomed search, something like Charlie Brown's search for a perfect Christmas tree.

This year was no different than usual as far as finding the trillium, but the time was not really lost, for I finally was able to add the golden-winged warbler to my lifetime bird list. A pair of these lovely, rare warblers were spotted in some bushes along an overgrown woods road. Hidden by the leaves, the male especially might almost have been mistaken for a chickadee except for the golden cap and the dull golden wing patch. But it was not really surprising that the search had good, although unplanned, results, for we have been told, "Seek and ye shall find."

And so I say to you: Ask, and you will receive, seek and you will find; knock and the door will be opened to you. For everyone who asks will receive, and he who seeks will find, and the door will be opened to anyone who knocks.

Luke 11:9-10

The Springtime of a Snapping Turtle

On a warm spring morning in early May I was busily cleaning out the springhouse when nearby, on the creek bank, I noticed a snapping turtle. Closer inspection revealed that it was a female turtle who had been laying eggs in a shallow hole dug in the gravelly bank. Now she was laboriously pushing dirt over them. If all goes well the baby turtles will probably hatch from the eggs in early autumn, close to the pleasant rippling water that will be the source of their sustenance and growth for the rest of their lives.

The snapping turtle is an important link in the chain of

life of our streams and ponds, but even I have to admit that the snapping turtle didn't get its name by sitting around looking sociable, and so I was relieved that Lira only inspected it in a gingerly sort of way, and then went off on other pursuits. Then I also left so that the turtle could finish covering over her eggs and slip back into the cool water, scented with mint and sweet flagg and the groundnut vine that trails along the banks, leaving the prospective babies in the most promising of locations with everything they will need close at hand.

How interesting and joyful a beautiful stream makes one's life—all of His animals and creatures, large and small, beautiful and homely (as I am afraid snapping turtle looks to most eyes, but to mine she looks just fine). God must have known we would all love a pure cool stream flowing through our lives, for even in the first garden, Eden, there was a stream.

A stream flowed in Eden and watered the garden; beyond Eden it divided into four rivers. The first river is the Pishon; it flows around the country of Havilah. (Pure gold is found there and also rare perfume and precious stones.) The second river is the Gihon; it flows around the country of Cush. The third river is the Tigris, which flows east of Assyria, and the fourth river is the Euphrates.

Genesis 2:10-14

Coveting Our Neighbor's Ox

On a dusky, overcast morning the first thing I hear when I step outdoors is the beautiful spring song of the cardinal coming from the trees beside a small stream. All winter I have heard the clear whistled "whe-at" of the cardinal who was often up in the larch trees picking out the tiny seeds from the cones. He is always a wonderful sight, his blazing red feathers so colorful against the drifts of white snow. And he also feeds on the seeds I scatter for the birds beneath a cedar tree in the yard, along with his loving mate who is dove-colored, with a softer red on her crest and wings and tail.

But now he is singing a more complicated arrangement, suitable to the new season when the hours of daylight are much longer, when every rivulet is brimming over with melt-water, and once again he wants to reassure his mate that she is matchless in his eyes. (Although, to be perfectly honest, I have sometimes seen him crowd her away from his beloved sunflower seeds if he is feeling especially possessive of them.)

The song of the cardinal is so pleasing, so joyful, so just plain wonderful. Sometimes we think God only commands us to do grim, difficult things, like not coveting our neighbor's spouse or his ox, but maybe his commands also cover such things as taking time to listen to the strains of melody that come from his own creation, the cardinal. At the same time that God spreads his world before us for our contemplation and highest enjoyment, it must be that he also wants us to tend the earth with loving hands. We could lose our birthright, as Esau did, if we give up the difficult struggle to protest our beautiful land.

I am here on earth for just a little while: do not hide your commands from me.

Psalm 119:19

Dreaming Up Blueberries

Blueberries do not grow wild in my section of the north country, but I had always wanted to try to raise them. I had been brought up on my mother's stories of her childhood in the Taconic Mountains of New York state where you could go out on any summer's day and easily pick a pailful of blue-berries. As a matter of fact, whole families often spent the entire summer picking blueberries, selling them at about 8 cents to 10 cents a quart to wholesale buyers who came through the mountain villages, purchasing the berries and reselling them in towns and cities. My mother who, with the aid of scholarships, worked her way through Cornell, had quite a little nest egg from the blueberry sales by the time she entered college.

So finally, several years ago I started a blueberry bed even though some very skilled gardeners among my acquaintances said that they had tried and failed with blueberries. Before actually starting, however, I gave a great deal of thought to blueberries, I meditated about blueberries, I dreamed about them. (I was wide-awake, but still dreaming.) I knew that these failed blueberry gardeners would know about aluminum sulfate, an essential to growing them in many places, and that they were such fine gardeners that I could not hope to surpass their accomplishments unless I was able to think of some missing element that the blueberries needed but were not getting in the aforementioned situations. Finally, something, perhaps the wind, seemed to carry the message, "Pine trees." Blueberries and pine trees seemed to go together in my memory. In earlier years our family had sometimes driven to an area about 30 miles south of here where the berries grow naturally and landowners often allowed pickers on their land for a charge of about 10 cents a quart. Pine trees often shaded both berries and pickers. Pine Plains, a sandy and piney area north of Watertown, had been a haunt for blueberry pickers for many years until the army took it over for a military encampment. I accidentally heard about one local horticulturist who did have thriving blueberries. I asked his wife if there happened to be any pines near her husband's berries and she said that there were. And my neighbors at a camp down my old road had set out a few bushes in the edge of a pine plantation and they were very productive.

So I thought perhaps the blueberries in some way needed pine trees, and I made my initial bed near a large pine tree, the only one available in a suitable spot. I spaded up the area, mixing in some light sandy gravel, peat moss and aluminum sulfate. After the bushes were set out I mulched them heavily with pine needles I had picked up by the bas-

96

ketful in the nearby pine plantations, and through the summer watered the blueberry bed frequently. The bushes seemed happy with their station in life and even during the first summer I had a cup full of the delicious, huge, cool blueberries. The handsome bushes are also good ornamental plantings for the yard. In the springtime there are the lovely bell shaped pinkish-white flowers, all summer the foliage is a thick, shining deep green, and in the fall the leaves turn to a fiery crimson.

A year or two later I was not surprised to read in a scientific magazine that the roots of pine trees do secrete a substance beneficial to blueberries. A little patient dreaming, wondering and thinking can be the beginning of a precious crop!

Be patient, then, my brothers, until the Lord comes. See how patient a farmer is as he waits for his land to produce precious crops.

James 5:7

Eyesight

When I visit the spring this morning to fill a jug with the clear, fast-flowing water, I find a little red-backed salamander entrapped in the pail that is positioned under the outlet pipe. The water constantly flows through the pipe into the pail where the overflow drains off into a ditch that carries it down to the main creek.

Some years, at least in the spring, summer and fall, I rescue salamanders almost every day from this pail. I have never really understood how so many of them get swept through the pipes that finally dump them into this container. They can withstand complete or partial submersion in the water for a while, but eventually they need to be rescued. It probably has something to do with their ability to breathe. (Salamanders breathe by means of gills, or lungs, or through the skin on the inside of the mouth.)

In the past I have noticed that when I happened to find a little salamander on the slab of cement, where the pail sits, he wriggles wildly around until his head is under a fallen leaf or debris of some kind, peering out through natural openings in this camouflage with a bright, dark eye. He seems to think he is safe if he can just get his head under cover. And perhaps he is, for then there are no bright, dark, *alive* eyes, so full of shy, quiet life to give away his secret hiding place. There are no fallen leaves around today, so after I pick the salamander out of the pail and place him on the concrete, I collect several moist golden dandelion flowers and lay them over his head. I hope they will make him feel happy and safe.

Your eyes are like a lamp for the body. When your eyes are sound, your whole body is full of light; but when your eyes are no good, your whole body will be in darkness.

Luke 11:34

Gateways

Some years ago we had a gateway near the barn that led to a small meadow where cows were sometimes pastured along a quiet stream. Wild strawberries were always plentiful along the edges of the meadow, glowing like rubies down in the grass. The gateway had no real gate but it was closed by a complex system of poles and some sagging strands of barbed wire. One time a visiting aunt from the midwest wanted to go through the gateway and go berrying in the sunlit meadow adorned with countless wild flowers. My parents took the makeshift gate entirely apart to let her through.

Later I questioned my mother in a rather querulous way I am afraid: "Nobody ever took that gateway apart for me when I went berrying. I always had to crawl through the barbed wire as best I could." My mother smiled with amusement and said, "Well, I'm afraid she wouldn't have been able to get through at all if we had not taken it down."

Jesus tells us that he is the gate, that he is all-sufficient for our salvation and that he will not turn us away when we come to him. When we pass through we will find pleasant pastures where our needs will be supplied by our Savior Jesus Christ.

I am the gate. Whoever comes in by me will be saved; he will come in and go out and find pasture.

John 10:9

The author lives in upper New York state deep in the heart of the rural countryside she loves. She is a graduate of Cornell University with a degree in botany and natural sciences. For several years she wrote a monthly column, "Parables from the Bittersweet Garden," for her parish newsletter. She also contributed the December, 1986, and January, 1987, meditations for *Forward Day by Day.*

Most of her work over the years has been farm related— maintaining a small dairy herd, raising strawberries and vegetables for sale (dried beans were one of her favorite crops), and making maple sugar, some of which found its way to such distant places as California, Germany and England. The bittersweet she planted is still sold or given away for autumn decorations. Now her life is centered in a small cabin where she lives and writes. The heart of the cabin is a little black air-tight stove with a ceramic glass door, made in Quebec "where winters are really winters." It brings warmth, safety and comfort to the country home where she tries to express through her writings her deep reverence for God and love of the wild and not-so-wild outdoor places.

Drawings on the cover and within this book are by Willie Hillenbrand